WALES BY BUS

Wales by Bus

Alastair Ross

ISBN: 1-84527-096-7

Cover design: Sian Parri

Published in 2006
by Gwasg Carreg Gwalch,
12 Iard yr Orsaf, Llanrwst, Wales LL26 0EH
☎ 01492 642031   🖷 01492 641502
✆ books@carreg-gwalch.co.uk   Website: www.carreg-gwalch.co.uk

Great care has been taken to be accurate. But neither the author
nor the publisher can accept any responsibility for errors or their
consequences. In any case, information can change.
If in doubt, always check first.

About the author
Alastair Ross is originally from Pontypool, Gwent. He has
enjoyed the adventure of exploring Wales by bus ever since
childhood. He works as a secondary school teacher.

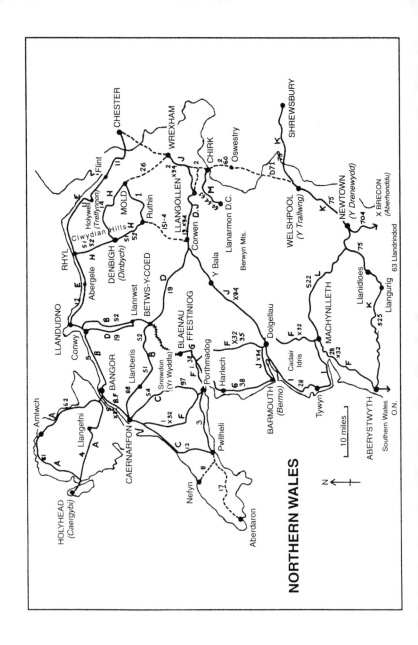

NORTHERN WALES

Contents

Introduction and General Information 10
How to use this book 12
Bus Services in Wales 14
Changes and Information 18
Rover tickets 20
Bus services in scenic or tourist areas 25
Index to Services 28

The Journeys

A A Circuit of Anglesey – the Mother of Wales
   Bangor – Holyhead – Amlwch - Bangor 34
B The Heart Of Gwynedd
   Llandudno – Betws y coed – Llanberis – Caernarfon
   – Llandudno 46
C The Lleyn Peninsula
   Caernarfon – Beddgelert - Porthmadog – Pwllheli
   – Caernarfon 60
D From the Conwy to the Dee
   Llandudno – Betws-y- coed - Llangollen 70
E The Northern Coast
   Llandudno – Rhyl – Chester 80
F TrawsCambria North
   Bangor – Caernarfon – Porthmadog – Dolgellau
   – Machynlleth – Aberystwyth 90
G The Meirionnydd Coast
   Barmouth – Harlech - Blaenau Ffestiniog 102
H The Clwydian Hills and the Vale of Clwyd
   Rhyl – Denbigh – Ruthin – Mold – Denbigh – Rhyl 110
I From the Dyfi to the Mawddach
   Machynlleth – Tywyn - Dolgellau 120

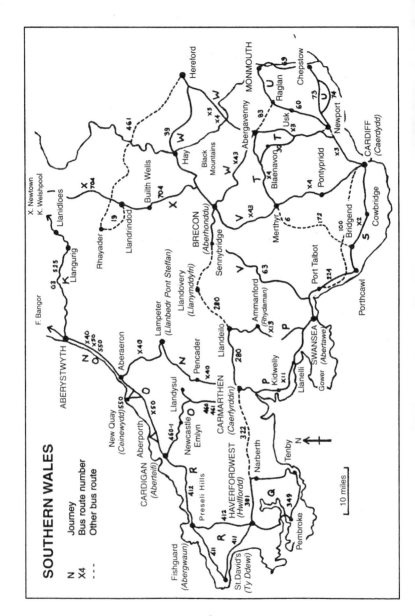

SOUTHERN WALES

N   Journey
X4   Bus route number
- - - Other bus route

10 miles

J Through the Heart of Northern Wales
Wrexham – Llangollen – Bala – Dolgellau – Barmouth .126

K Across the Cambrian Mountains
Shrewsbury - Welshpool – Newtown – Llanidloes
- Aberystwyth 136

L Rivers and Rebels
Newtown – Caersws – Carno - Machynlleth 148

M The Ceiriog Valley
Chirk – Llanarmon Dyffryn Ceiriog 156

N TrawsCambria South
Aberystwyth – Lampeter – Carmarthen 164

O The Romans, the Normans and a Legendary Wizard
Carmarthen – Cardigan –Aberystwyth 172

P Carmarthenshire
Carmarthen – Llandeilo – Swansea – Llanelli
– Carmarthen 180

Q South Pembrokeshire
Haverfordwest – Narberth – Tenby – Pembroke
– Haverfordwest 190

R St David's and the Pembrokeshire Coast
Cardigan – Fishguard – St David's – Haverfordwest –
Cardigan 200

S Two Cities
Cardiff – Porthcawl - Swansea 210

T The Valleys of the South East
Cardiff – Merthyr – Abergavenny – Cardiff 218

U Forts and Castles in Border Country
Monmouth – Chepstow – Newport - Monmouth 228

V Around the Beacons
Swansea – Brecon – Merthyr 240

W The Black Mountains
Brecon – Hay – Hereford – Abergavenny – Brecon ..250

X Through Powys
Newtown – Llandrindod – Builth Wells – Brecon 260

Introduction and General Information

The Freedom of Wales

One Saturday morning in May 2005, I stood on Llangollen's historic bridge, one of the supposed 'Seven Wonders of Wales', waiting for the bus to Barmouth. The newly launched X94 TrawsCambria service arrived from Wrexham, well patronised by shoppers and students heading for a day out by the sea. Our journey followed the Dee valley to Bala and on across the backbone of Wales to Dolgellau, before following the northern shore of the Mawddach estuary to smell the spray of the Irish Sea. I had an hour to explore Barmouth before travelling north along the coast of Cardigan Bay. Another hour in Harlech allowed a visit to the dramatic castle before taking a bus on to Blaenau Ffestiniog, in the heart of slate country. I used the train service along the picturesque Conwy Valley line to reach Llanrwst, followed by a modest stroll across the valley to Trefriw. I returned to Betws-y-coed by bus in time for a meal, before taking the last service directly back to Llangollen. The price of this marathon was just £4.95, the cost of a standard adult Red Rover day ticket, valid through much of NW Wales.

Bus travel is often seen as neither fashionable nor efficient. This particular day out may serve to illustrate the inadequacy of such stereotyping. All but one of the journeys was on a modern, state of the art bus. Even the exception was perfectly acceptable. None were overcrowded and some were almost empty. The rides offered incomparable views of a dramatic landscape of mountains, forest, moorland and sea. Services were regular and information readily available. I could design my own tour rather than succumb to the slavery of an official coach tour.

The bus network in Wales invites exploration. Buses serve almost every corner of the country. The Welsh Assembly Government and the local authorities have been proactive in developing new regional and local routes with operators. The assembly has funded new vehicles and expanded the national network of TrawsCambria routes. If you are a pensioner or other eligible resident in Wales, you have all this for free with the Cerdyn Cymru pass. But even if your pension is many years away, or you live elsewhere, the network is very economical with a range of rovers valid for a day or a longer period.

The prospect of a journey always sends a tingle down the spine. The idea of an adventure always inspires a sense of freedom. There is plenty to find in familiar places as well as new ones. Buses offer an easy, flexible and cheap way to see nearly every corner of the country. The aim of this book is to show how the Welsh bus network can be used for an odyssey of discovery. It does so simply by describing a range of bus journeys throughout Wales, with a map, outline of the route pattern, list of places of interest and description of the journey itself. Of course, these are only examples. You can mix and match parts of the journeys to form your own itinerary. Or perhaps you will be inspired to make up your own, with the easy-to-use, accessible information now available. There are infinite possibilities.

How to Use this Book

The book is divided into 24 'Journeys' covering all parts of Wales. Each Journey is given a letter corresponding to the chapter that describes it. Use of letters avoids confusion with bus route numbers.

The Reference Maps
Two reference maps show the location of these Journeys. One map covers northern Wales (page 6) and the other southern Wales (page 8). Some of the Journeys are circular tours, which start and finish at the same location. These involve a number of different bus trips. Other Journeys are linear, finishing at a different place from their start. The reference maps also indicate bus route numbers. Of course, you can make up your own tour by combining sections of different Journeys shown on the map. Hatched lines indicate 'links', connecting bus routes which are not described in the text but which may be useful.

The Index of Routes
This table lists routes described in the book in numerical order. It gives an outline of the route's frequency, the operator, valid rover tickets and the Journey in which the route appears. See page 28.

The Journeys
Each chapter covers a particular Journey. It includes a description of the route and points of interest. At the end is a summary of route information, including details of the route pattern and frequency. There is a list of selected places of interest with website and telephone contact

details. I have also added briefly some suggestions for walks in many of the areas covered.

Timetables

I have given an outline of the service frequency for each bus service. I have not included specific timetable information. The reason for this is probably obvious - it becomes out of date very quickly. However, getting detailed information is easy. See the section on Changes and Information on page 18.

'Weekday frequency' means the normal Monday – Friday daytime pattern. Saturdays may vary, though usually not much. On most rural services there are no evening buses. Where there is a service, I have indicated this in the Index of Routes.

'Sunday frequency' means the normal Sunday daytime service. On most rural services there are no evening buses. Where there is a service, I have indicated this in the Index of Routes.

Bus Services in Wales

All change?

Much is made of the fact that, since deregulation in 1986, bus companies can change their timetables at short notice. And they do. However, the overall service pattern and frequency is generally much more stable. Although there have been changes over the years, for better and worse, there are remarkable similarities with the historic pattern. As a child I rode on Red and White's hourly Cardiff-Gloucester No 73 service. It still runs hourly and with the same number, though now from Newport and with Stagecoach as the operator. Similarly I remember Newport Transport's No 2 bus which still runs to Caerleon, though every 15 minutes rather than half-hourly, and with a string of idiosyncratic suffix letters. Similar correspondence can be found throughout Wales.

In the days of the National Bus Company, Wales was effectively divided into three segments. The southeast was the shared territory of Red and White, based in Chepstow, and Western Welsh, whose head office was in Cardiff. Most of the services in the Gwent valleys were run jointly. In the latter days of nationalisation, the two companies merged to form National Welsh. In a similar way, two companies, United Welsh and South Wales Transport, jointly operated most of the routes around Swansea, including the city services. Most of the remainder of Wales was the huge empire of Crosville Motor Services, the Chester based company that also ran through Cheshire and south Merseyside. Since privatisation a shadowy image of this pattern has remained. The three biggest UK bus groups, which together control 60% of the bus market, now have one each of these historic fiefdoms. First Group, Britain's biggest bus company, operates in western Wales. Stagecoach took control of the old Red and White /Western Welsh area in the south and east. Arriva run the Welsh area of Crosville's operations.

There are differences. The Big Three do not operate the extensive network of local services that once existed. Commercial companies can only run economically viable services. Others, deemed socially necessary, become the responsibility of the local council and are put out to tender. In some areas, this is the majority of services. It is often the smaller independent companies who have been able to offer more competitive bids and have won the tenders. Some of these operations have built substantial businesses from this system. Rivalry for lucrative tenders can be acute. Indeed, I have visited one small Scottish island where the two bus operators have not talked to each other for years as a result. But even before the era of deregulation, independent operators have been a feature of rural areas. They continue to offer a substantial range of services and some, such as Richards Brothers in western Wales, are the major operators in parts of the country. A largely rural country, Wales was never a stronghold of municipal operators. However, Cardiff and Newport both had council operated transport services, now transformed into Cardiff Bus and Newport Transport. Since the 1960s, Cardiff's buses transmuted from maroon and cream, through a shade of sickly orange, to the present turquoise based livery. Newport has stuck with its traditional green and cream. Both have successfully avoided takeovers from larger groups. Smaller ex-municipal operators have survived in the valleys, though in some places, such as Merthyr, they have been swallowed up.

The other change is the demise of the double decker.

Over the past few years both Swansea and Cardiff have converted entirely to single deck operation, though a few elderly orange two-deck relics hang on in Cardiff. Newport Transport is the only Welsh bus company that has bought new double deckers over recent years and continues to deploy them systematically. In the rest of the country, you will hardly see a double deck vehicle. Occasional sightings are limited to Aberystwyth or to the open-air tourist variety in Llandudno. One of the latter does go all the way to the foot of Snowdon (see Journey C).

TrawsCambria

One of the most exciting developments in recent years has been the promotion and expansion of the TrawsCambria network. Until 2004 the TrawsCambria name was given to a single bus service that ran once a day between north and south Wales, stopping for lunch in Aberystwyth. Although there were a couple of supplementary journeys, it was infrequent and very slow. The Welsh Assembly Government has encouraged the development of the network over the past few years and the north-south service now operates in two sections: Bangor – Aberystwyth and Aberystwyth – Carmarthen /Cardiff. The northern section runs every two hours, with other services supplementing this frequency for most of the way. The southern section runs hourly as far as Carmarthen railway station, the railhead for Swansea and Cardiff. Two buses each day extend to Cardiff. The Wrexham-Barmouth service has been included in the TrawsCambria network as the X94 with an improved timetable and new vehicles. An X50 has been established between Aberystwyth and Cardigan, though the present timetable is rather odd. Early in 2006, a new service 704

16

was introduced between Brecon and Newtown, filling an acute gap in Wales' bus network. Other developments are uncertain, but may include revamping the services between Cardigan and Haverfordwest, Shrewsbury and Llanidloes/Aberystwyth. Possible new routes include Welshpool – Wrexham – Rhyl and Brecon – Abergavenny – Newport. It is possible that TrawsCambria services may be renumbered into a 700 series rather than using an X prefix.

Changes and Information

Like a telephone directory, changes affect a book such as this, even before it is published. However, although bus numbers and operators may alter from time to time, much of the present pattern is likely to remain. I have tried to organise the information in such a way as to minimise the propensity to obsolescence! Even if a route number changes, the details of the journey will not be transformed so superficially. Hopefully, it will provide useful background and details for years to come. To find out detailed travel information, you have a variety of sources.

Traveline
Details of all Welsh bus services are available from the Traveline website, www.traveline-cymru.org.uk. You can also phone this service on 0870 608 2 608, though regrettably, unlike the train enquiry line, you pay a national rate even for local enquiries. The line is open from 0700 until 2200 daily. If you're dialling from outside Wales, dial 4 as soon as the recorded message starts, and you will be connected to Traveline Cymru rather than your own local enquiry centre.

Local Authorities
Local authorities produce excellent maps and timetable booklets, though their availability is sometimes variable. You can contact local authorities during office hours on the numbers below. They jointly fund an outstanding overall map and guide to buses throughout Wales, produced by the Wales Tourist Board.

Anglesey	01248-752459
	www.anglesey.gov.uk
Caerphilly	01495-235223
	www.caerphilly.gov.uk
Cardiff	029-2087 3252
	www.cardiff.gov.uk
Carmarthenshire	01267-231817
	www.carmarthenshire.gov.uk
Ceredigion	01970-633555
	www.ceredigion.gov.uk
Conwy	01492-575412
	www.conwy.gov.uk
Denbighshire	01824-706968
	www.denbighshire.gov.uk
Flintshire	01352-704035
	www.flintshire.gov.uk
Gwent Joint PT unit*	01495-355444
	www.blaenau-gwent.gov.uk
Gwynedd	01286-697535
	www.gwynedd.gov.uk
Pembrokeshire	01437-764551
	www.pembrokeshire.gov.uk
Powys	0845-6076060
	www.powys.gov.uk
Rhondda Cynon Taf	01443-494816
	www.rhondda-cynon-taff.gov.uk
Vale of Glamorgan	01446-704687
	www.valeofglamorgan.gov.uk
Wrexham	01978-266166
	www.wrexham.gov.uk

* Includes Blaenau Gwent, Monmouthshire, Newport and Torfaen.

Rover Tickets

There is a wide range of rover tickets covering the whole country. These offer outstanding value for money and they may even be cheaper than a straightforward return. I have included 2005-06 prices to give an idea of cost. Prices have been very stable in recent years, but please bear in mind that there may be changes in costs and conditions. The range of tickets may also change. Letters after the title indicate the code used in the Route Information table for each Journey (eg RR). In all cases please check conditions before you travel; there may be restrictions at certain times of day.

Freedom of Wales Flexipass
There are a number of options: an All Wales version and regional clones that offer travel in the north or south of the country.

All Wales (FPN,FPS)
All timetabled rail services in Wales, including the line from Chester via Shrewsbury to Newport, and the service between Newport and Lydney. Almost all bus services in the whole country. Also valid on the Ffestiniog and Welsh Highland railways. Discounts on many attractions.

Any 8 consecutive days bus and 4 days train within this period.
Peak season:
£55.00 adult   £36.50 child or railcard discount
Off peak:
£45.00 adult   £29.70 child or railcard discount

Any 15 consecutive days bus and 8 days train within this period.
Peak season:
£92.00 adult   £60.70 child or railcard discount
Off peak:
£75.00 adult   £49.50 child or railcard discount

North and Mid Wales (FPN)
All timetabled rail services bounded by Chester, Crewe, Shrewsbury and Aberystwyth. Almost all bus services in North and Mid Wales. Also valid on the Ffestiniog and Welsh Highland railways. Discounts on many attractions.

Bus and rail on any 3 days out of 7.
£30.00 adult   £19.80 child

South Wales (FPS)
All timetabled rail services in South Wales, as far as Hereford and Lydney. Also Swansea to Craven Arms and Shrewsbury. Almost all bus services in South and much of Mid Wales. Discounts on many attractions.

Any 7 consecutive days bus and 3 days train within this period.

Peak season:	£35.00 adult	£23.10 child
Off peak:	£30.00 adult	£19.80 child

For further details visit www.walesflexipass.co.uk or telephone 0870 9000777. Tickets available at staffed railway stations in Wales and many major stations in England.

Red Rover (RR)
Extensive one-day travel in NW Wales. Buses 1-99 in Gwynedd and Anglesey. Buses X19 to Llangollen, 48, 64, 75 and 84 in Conwy. Also TrawsCambria services X32

Bangor – Aberystwyth and X94 Wrexham - Barmouth. Valid on trains between Blaenau Ffestiniog and Llandudno only. Buy on the bus.

£4.95 adult   £2.45 child

Snowdon Sherpa Day Ticket (SS)
Day travel around Snowdon. Buy on the bus.

£4.00 adult

Vale Rider (VR)
One day's unlimited travel on many inland services in Denbighshire, including some cross border routes. Buy on the bus.

£3.50 adult   £1.75 child/OAP   £7.00 family

Conexxions Day 1
Valid on most bus services in Flintshire and on the Clwydian Sunday buses. Buy on the bus.

£3.50 adult   £1.75 child   £8.00 family

West Wales Day Rover (WW)
Almost all buses in Carmarthenshire, Pembrokeshire and Ceredigion, including services into Swansea from these counties. Buy on the bus.

£5.00 adult   £3.70 child   £2.50 accompanied child

South Wales Network Rider Ticket (NR)
One day's travel on Bebb, Cardiff Bus, Chepstow Classic Bus, Glyn Williams, Islwyn Borough, Newport Transport, Shamrock, Stagecoach in S Wales and Welcome. Covers a wide area of SE Wales. Buy on the bus.

£5.40 adult   £3.30 child   £10.80 family

Cardiff Valley Lines Day Explorer

Available for one day on local train services up the valleys from Cardiff. Also to Penarth, Barry, Maesteg. Valid on all Stagecoach in S Wales buses. Buy at local staffed train stations.

£7.00 adult   £3.50 child

Single Company Rovers

Most operators offer day tickets for unlimited travel on their own buses. Some offer tickets for longer periods.

Arriva Cymru has a range of tickets. Be careful if using the 75 Shrewsbury-Llanidloes service as this is operated by Arriva Midlands North.

First Day South and West Wales allows unlimited travel on First buses locally, but not the Shuttle 100 between Cardiff and Swansea.

Stagecoach, Cardiff Bus and Richards Brothers also offer day tickets.

Cerdyn Cymru

Of course, if you are over 60 (or otherwise eligible) and resident in Wales, you will probably not need to be told that virtually every bus journey in Wales is open to you free of charge. You need a Cerdyn Cymru pass, which can be obtained through your local council. These passes are also valid across the border to places such as Gloucester, Hereford and Chester, provided you get on the bus in Wales.

Tocyn Taith (TT)

Intoduced in 2006, this ticket offers joint rail and bus travel through northern Wales. There are 6 zones:

- **A** Anglesey
- **G** Gwynedd
- **C** Conwy
- **D** Denbighshire
- **F** Flintshire
- **W** Wrexham
- **Z** Chester

A ticket is valid for a full day with no time restrictions 2 zones costs £6, 3 zones £10, 4 zones £15 and all zones £20. It is excellent value.

The Gwynedd zone extends into Anglesey as far as Llangefni & Amlwch. It also allows travel by train or bus to Aberystwyth.

The Wrexham zone allows travel to Gobowen and Oswestry.

Available on trains & buses.

Bus Services in Scenic or Tourist Areas

Snowdonia

The well-established Snowdon Sherpa network serves the areas around Snowdon. Many services run all week and all year round, though the pattern and frequency varies.

S1	Llanberis – Pen-y-pass
S2	Llanrwst – Pen-y-pass. Some buses from Llandudno in summer.
S4	Caernarfon – Beddgelert – Pen-y-pass
S6	Bangor – Bethesda – Pen-y-pass/ Betws-y-coed
S96	Porthmadog – Beddgelert – Rhyd-ddu
S97/97	Porthmadog – Beddgelert

Snowdon Sherpa Day Ticket available on all these services. Red Rover valid on all services.

For more details www.gwynedd.gov.uk/bwsgwynedd

Brecon Beacons

Beacons Bus operates every Sunday and Bank Holiday Monday during the summer period. There are services to Brecon from Cardiff, Newport, Swansea, Bridgend, Abergavenny and Carmarthen. Most operate once a day in each direction. There are also some local services around Llanthony, Hay, Talybont and the Mountain Centre.

Beacons Bus All Day Ticket is available for £5.50 adult, £3.75 child and £11.00 family. Some buses carry bicycles.

For more details contact 01873-853254 or www.visitbreconbeacons.com

Pembrokeshire Coast

Pembrokeshire Coastal Bus Services are provided by a partnership of local agencies. Buses operate along coastal sections of the national park enabling linear walks or other outings. They run daily from May to September. There are buses on services 387, 404 and 405 on three days a week out of season. Routes are outlined below. Buses travel via coastal villages rather than along a direct route. Some of these services could be combined with the direct services in Journey R to make a circular trip.

387	Coastal Cruiser	Pembroke – Angle
400	Puffin Shuttle	St David's – Milford Haven
403	Celtic Coaster	St David's area
404	Strumble Shuttle	Fishguard – St David's
405	Poppit Rocket	Cardigan – Fishguard

For more details contact the Travel Line on 0870 608 2 608 or visit www.pembrokeshiregreenways.co.uk

Clwydian Hills

Sunday and Bank Holiday services focus on Loggerheads Country Park, near Mold. Buses from Llangollen, Rhyl, Prestatyn, Mold, Flint and Chester arrive here. Other services link with Betws-y-coed and Barmouth. You can join together various routes to create an extensive tour. Buy on the bus.

A Clwydian Day Ranger Ticket covers the network.
£3.00 adult   £1.50 child/OAP   £6.00 family
Conexxions Day 1 tickets also valid.

For more details contact 01352-704035
or visit www.flintshire.gov.uk

Gower

The Gower Explorer network is operated by Pullman Coaches and funded by Swansea Council. One commercial route, service 14, is operated by First Cymru and serves Mumbles, Bishopston and Pennard Cliffs. Other Pullman buses serve most parts of Gower daily and quite frequently. City service 2 operates frequently between Swansea and Mumbles.

Pullman Day Rider tickets and the First day Swansea Bay day ticket both offer coverage of Gower and the Swansea area. Buy on the bus.

For more details contact Traveline 0870 608 2 608 or visit www.traveline-cymru.org.uk

Cardiff

Cardiff Bus operates frequent services throughout the city and to Barry and Penarth. The hub of the network is the Central Bus Station in Wood Street, right next to Central Station. Service 6, the Bay Express, goes from the back of the railway station to Cardiff Bay every 10 minutes. Buses 8 and 9 also serve Cardiff Bay from Wood Street every 15 minutes. The National History Museum of Wales is served by the 32 to St Fagans every hour.

City Rider is a one-day ticket valid on Cardiff Bus services in Cardiff and Penarth.

£3.50 adult   £2.30 child   £7.00 family
South Wales Network Rider also valid.

For more details visit www.cardiff.gov.uk/travel

INDEX TO SERVICES

The list below is a summary of the main services included in this book. More details are included in each Journey. Please note that SERVICES CHANGE. Buses may run more frequently over some sections of the route and other services may also exist. Operators may change, especially where the service is provided under contract. For full timetable details always check with the operator, or the Traveline. See the section 'Changes and Information' on page 18 for details of how to contact information providers.

No.	Route	Journey	Operator	Rover tickets	Weekday frequency#	Sunday frequency
1	Chester - Wrexham	link	AC	FPN,TT	10 min*	Hourly*
1	Bangor/Caernarfon - Blaenau Ffestiniog	F	E	FPN,RR,TT	Hourly*	Occasional
1/2	Ruthin - Mold	H	G	FPN,VR,TT	1-2 hours	No service
2	Newport - Caerleon	U	NT	FPS,NR	15 min*	30 min*
2	Wrexham - Oswestry	link	AC	FPN,TT	30 min	Hourly
3	Porthmadog - Pwllheli	C	AC/C	FPN,RR,TT	Apx.30 min*	2 hourly
4	Bangor - Holyhead	A	AC	FPN,RR,TT	30 min*	No service
5	Wrexham - Llangollen	J	AC/G/B	FPN,TT	15/30 min*	Hourly*
5/9A	Caernarfon - Llandudno	C	AC,KMP	FPN,RR,TT	30 min*	Hourly*
6	Merthyr - Aberdare	link	S	FPS,NR	30 min	5 journeys
8	Pwllheli - Nefyn	C	N	FPN,RR,TT	Aprox.hourly*	occasional
11/A	Rhyl - Chester	E	AC	FPN,TT	30 min*	2 hourly*
12	Llandudno - Rhyl	E	AC	FPN,TT	10 min*	30 min*
12	Pwllheli- Caernarfon	C	CT/BW	FPN,RR,TT	Hourly*	3 journeys

14/A	Mold - Denbigh	H	G	FPN,VR,TT	Hourly	No service
17	Pwllheli - Aberdaron	U	AC	FPN,RR,TT	Aprox.ev 90min	No service
19/X19	Llandudno - Betws-y-Coed	D	AC	FPN,RR,TT	Hourly*	Hourly to Llanrwst only*
X19	Llandudno - Llangollen	D	AC	FPN,RR	4 journeys	2 journeys
19	Llandrindod Wells - Rhayader	link	CG	FPS	6 journeys	No service
26	Wrexham - Mold	link	AC	FPN,TT	Hourly	No service
28	Aberystwyth - Dolgellau	I	AC	FPN,TT	2 hourly*	3 journeys Mach-Dolgellau
30	Brynmawr - Newport	T	S	FPS,NR	Hourly	No service
30	Newport - Cardiff	link	NT/CB	FPS,NR	20 min*	Hourly*
35	Dolgellau - Blaenau Ffestiniog	F	AC	FPN,RR,TT	Apx.2 hourly	See Journey F
38	Barmouth - Blaenau Ffestiniog	G	E	FPN,RR,TT	Apx. hourly	Limited ser from Harlech
39	Brecon - Hereford	W	S	FPS	7 journeys	2 journeys+
51-52	Rhyl - Denbigh++	H	AC	FPN,VR,TT	20 min*	Hourly*
60	Newport - Monmouth	U	HH	FPS,NR	2 hourly	No service
60	Oswestry - Llanarmon DC	M	G	FPN,TT	2 hourly to Glyn Ceiriog	No service
61	Holyhead - Amlwch	A	LL	FPN,RR,TT	Apx. 2 hourly	4 journeys
62	Bangor - Amlwch	A	AC	FPN,RR,TT	30 min*	2 hourly*
63	Swansea - Brecon	V	S	FPS,NR	3 journeys	No service
64	Llangollen - Glyn Ceiriog	M	B	FPN,TT	8 journeys	No service
65	Wrexham - Llanarmon DC	M	G	FPN,TT	4 journeys	No service
69	Monmouth - Chepstow	U	CC	FPS,NR	2 hourly*	2 hourly
73	Gloucester - Newport	U	S	FPS,NR	Hourly	No service
74	Chepstow - Newport	U	S	FPS,NR	Hourly*	2 hourly

75	Shrewsbury - Llanidloes	K	AMN	FPN	7 jnys-some chg N'town	No service
83	Abergavenny - Monmouth	link	Various	FPS,NR	2 hourly	2 hourly
88/9A	Llanberis - Caernarfon	C	KMP	FPN,RR,TT	30 min*	Hourly
97	Bedgelert - Porthmadog	C	E	FPN,RR,SS,TT	2 hourly	3 journeys
100	Cardiff - Swansea	S	FC	FPS	30 min	5 journeys
152	Denbigh/Ruthin - Corwen/Llangollen	link	G	FPN,VR,TT	Aprox 2 hourly	
172	Aberdare - Pontypridd - Porthcawl	link	S	FPS,NR	Hourly	4 journeys
224	Swansea - Porthcawl	S	FC	FPS	Hourly	No service
280	Carmarthen - Llandovery	P	FC	FPS,WW	7 journeys	No service
322	Carmarthen - Haverfordwest	link	SX	FPS,WW	2 journeys	No service
349	Haverfordwest - Tenby	Q	FC	FPS,WW	Hourly	2-4 journeys
381	Haverfordwest - Tenby	Q	SX	FPS,WW	Hourly	1 journey
411	Haverfordwest - Fishguard	R	RB	FPS,WW	2 hourly	No service
411	Haverfordwest - St David's	R	RB	FPS,WW	Hourly	4 journeys
412	Haverfordwest - Cardigan	R	RB	FPS,WW	Hourly	2 journeys
460/1	Carmarthen - Cardigan	O	RB/FC	FPS,WW	7 journeys*	No service
461	Hereford - Llandrindod Wells	link	SB	FPS	4 journeys	No service
522	Machynlleth - Newtown	L	LC	FPN	4 journeys	No service
525	Aberystwyth - Llanidloes	K	AC	FPN	3 journeys	No service
550	Cardigan - Aberystwyth	O	AC/RB	FPS,WW	2 hourly	2 hourly
704	Newtown - Brecon	X	S	FPS	2 hourly	No service
D71	Oswestry - Welshpool	link	TV	FPN	5 journeys	No service
S1	Llanberis - Pen-y-pass	C	KMP	FPN,RR,SS,TT	See Journey B	See Journey B

	Llandudno - Pen-y-pass	C	Various	FPN,RR,TT	See Journey B	See Journey B
S2	Caernarfon - Beddgelert	U	KMP	FPN,RR,TT	2 hourly	5 journeys
S4	Swansea - Carmarthen	P	FC	FPS,WW	30 min	No service
X11	Swansea - Llandeilo	P	FC	FPS,WW	Hourly - 30 min to A'fford	5 journeys
X13	Cardiff - Porthcawl	S	FC	FPS	30 min*	Hourly*
X2	Cardiff - Abergavenny - Hereford	W	S	FPS,NR	Aprox hourly	No service
X3/4	Cardiff - Abergavenny	T	S	FPS,NR	Hourly	No service
X3	Cardiff - Abergavenny	T	S	FPS,NR	Hourly	No service
X4	Bangor - Aberystwyth	F	AC/E	FPN,RR,TT	2 hourly	2 journeys
X32	Aberystwyth - Carmarthen	NO	FC/AC	FPS,WW	Hourly*	1 journey
X40	Abergavenny - Brecon - Merthyr	VW	SS	FPS	2 hrs-some ext to Cardiff	See Journey W
X43	Cardigan - Aberaeron - Aberystwyth	NO	RB	FPS,WW	8 jnys to Aberaeron	No service
X50	Wrexham - Barmouth	J	AC	FPN,RR,TT	Aprox 2 hours	4 journeys+
X94						

CODE

*   Evening service also operated (usually with a reduced frequency)

+   Operator may differ on Sunday

Based on Monday to Friday term time pattern. May vary on Saturdays or during school holidays

++   See Journey H for service Denbigh-Ruthin

31

OPERATORS

AC	Arriva Cymru
AMN	Arriva Midlands North
B	Bryn Melyn
BW	Berwyn
C	Caelloi
CB	Cardiff Bus
CC	Chepstow Classic Coaches
CG	Cross gates Coaches
CT	Clynnog & Trefor
E	Express Motors
FC	First Cymru
G	GHA Coaches
HH	HH Motors
LC	Lloyd's Coaches
N	Nefyn
NT	Newport Transport
S	Stagecoach in S Wales
SB	Sergeant Brothers
SS	Sixty Sixty Coaches
SX	Silcox
TV	Tanat Valley

ROVER TICKETS

For details of these please see the section 'Rover Tickets' in the introduction.

FPN	All Wales Freedom of Wales Flexipass and North and Mid Wales Flexi Rover

FPS	All Wales Freedom of Wales Flexipass and Freedom of South Wales Flexi Rover
NR	Network Rider
RR	Red Rover
SS	Snowdon Sherpa
TT	Tocyn Taith
VR	Vale Rider
WW	West Wales Rover

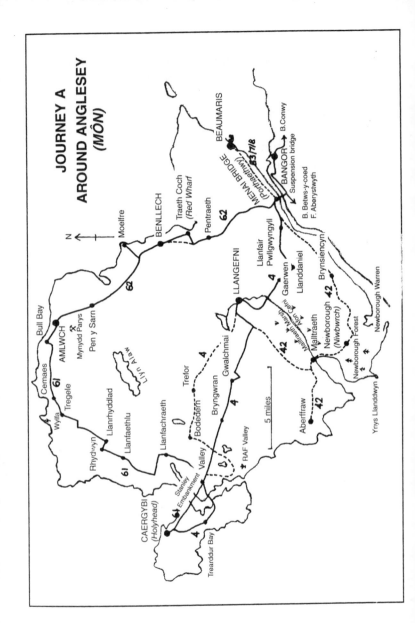

JOURNEY A
AROUND ANGLESEY
(MÔN)

Journey A: A Circuit of Anglesey – The 'Mother of Wales'

Bangor – Holyhead – Amlwch – Bangor

Surrounded by 125 miles of dunes and cliffs, Anglesey is sometimes referred to as the 'Mother of Wales', or the 'Breadbasket of Gwynedd'. The mountains of Snowdonia form a dramatic backdrop to a land of fertile farmland, interspersed with gorse-clad rocky knolls. Fifty windmills once powered machinery to grind the corn and, still today, natural power is harnessed at a wind farm in the centre of the island. Anglesey lies on the main route between Britain and Ireland. On a clear evening, half way across the sea from Ireland, you can see the distant glimmer of Dublin Bay behind at the same time as the reassuring flash of South Stack lighthouse ahead. A reminder that the sixty-mile voyage has always been a busy route for Celtic traders and for Viking raiders.

Bangor to Holyhead

The city of **Bangor** lies hidden in a bowl, just inland from the Menai straits, a position that saved it from marauding raiders long since. St Deiniol founded a monastery here around 525CE, naming his community after the 'bangor' or perimeter wall that surrounded the original settlement. Bangor's cathedral can lay claim to being the oldest diocesan see in Wales, although the present building dates from the 12th to 16th centuries and was much restored in the 19th. Bangor is also home to part of the University of Wales. Opened in 1884, it was the third college of the university after Aberystwyth and Cardiff, giving the north a seat of learning. The main building sits astride the ridge between the city and the sea. Down at the seafront, Bangor's pier was recently refurbished and allows pedestrians to walk half way across the Menai Straits towards Anglesey.

The first leg of our journey follows the line of the A5, Telford's turnpike road to Ireland, with a number of entertaining diversions. The main road is no longer the busy trunk route it once was. The A55 Expressway now flies across Anglesey, halving the journey time to the port. The original route, and the bus journey, is all the better for that.

Leaving Bangor, you climb through the outskirts and soon glimpse the **Menai Strait**, separating mainland Wales from Anglesey. The narrow crossing, no more than 300 metres at one point, is deceptively treacherous and its swirling currents and fast tidal races have always presented a major hazard to travellers. In 1785 a boat carrying 55 people became stranded on a sandbar in the strait and was then engulfed by the advancing tide. Rescue attempts failed and all but one lost their lives. After the Act of Union with Ireland in 1800, traffic to Holyhead increased and plans were drawn up for a permanent bridge. Built between 1819 and 1826, Thomas Telford's suspension bridge carries 579 feet of roadway at a height of over 100 feet above the water, high enough to allow high-masted ships to pass below.

Just a mile to the west is Britannia Bridge, built by Robert Stephenson in 1850, to carry the railway line across the Menai. In 1970 a fire, accidentally started by two boys, destroyed it. But it was rebuilt, this time with an upper deck to carry a second road crossing into Anglesey.

Passing through the town of Menai Bridge, the bus skirts above the northern shore of the strait and soon reaches **Llanfair Pwllgwyngyll**. As you approach the village, the Marquess of Anglesey's Column looms up on the right. Completed two years after the Battle of Waterloo (1815), the statue was added in 1860 giving a total height of 32 metres. It commemorates Henry William Paget, first Marquess of Anglesey, who was second in command to Wellington at the Battle of Waterloo in 1815. You can climb the 115 steps to enjoy panoramic views. The Marquess' home, Plas Menai, lies two miles to the south and is in the care of the National Trust. There are many places in Wales called Llanfair (St Mary's) but in the nineteenth century a local tailor hit on a novel way of distinguishing this one. He added several syllables to make the longest place name in Wales. Llanfairpwllgwyngyllgogerychyrndrobwllllantisilio-gogogoch means St Mary's church in the hollow of a white hazel tree near a fast whirlpool and the church of St Tysilio near a red cave. Once its name has been admired, there is little reason to stop in Llanfair Pwllgwyngyll, although a factory outlet offering the usual selection of cardigans, coffee table books and pot pourri is popular with coach tours.

The exact route of bus 4 across Anglesey varies according to the particular time you are travelling. All variations offer a pleasant traverse of the island. After visiting Llanddaniel and Gaerwen you drop down to the **Malltraeth Marsh**, or Cors Ddyga, a low-lying wetland that almost severs the island in two. In 1810 an embankment was built to exclude the sea and the river was later canalised, but much wetland still remains and is protected as a SSSI. As well as a range of plants, a wide variety of birds find protection and food in the marsh. Even the boom of the secretive bittern can occasionally be heard.

After crossing the Afon Cefni, the island's longest

river, the bus soon leaves the A5 to divert into **Llangefni**, its county town. Anglesey's capital is a bustling town, especially on market days. Nearby Oriel Ynys Mon, Anglesey's museum and art gallery offers displays on the island's history, culture and industry. Not far to the east, on the back road from Menai Bridge, lies the hamlet of Penmynydd. Now just a straggling collection of houses, it was the origin of the Tudor dynasty. Through a marriage in 1429, Owain Tudor of Penmynydd gained a loose claim to the English throne. This was exercised by his grandson Henry, who became Henry VII of England after victory in the Battle of Bosworth Field in 1485, the final act in the Wars of the Roses.

Most buses rejoin the A5 and continue across the interior of Anglesey through Gwalchmai and Bryngwran, though some operate by a more northerly route through Bodedern. All routes unite at **Valley** where the RAF base is home to the rescue service as well as being a west coast defence base. Instead of ploughing straight across the Stanley Embankment on the A5, the bus crosses over to Anglesey's satellite, Holy Island on Four Mile Bridge. The fact that you're actually crossing the Irish Sea at this point is hardly evident and you soon arrive in the charming seaside resort of Trearddur Bay, with houses dotted alongside a series of rocky pools facing southwest across the sea. It is not far from here to the busy port of Holyhead, terminus of the A5, the British road network and bus number 4.

Holyhead to Amlwch

The Welsh name for **Holyhead**, Caergybi (fort of Cybi), reveals two threads in the history of the town. Romans built a fort here in the third century to control the pirates at sea. The fort came to shelter a settlement around the parish church named after St Cybi who came here in the sixth century. Some of the original walls still stand. Holyhead became a major port for Ireland after the end of the eighteenth century. The arrival of Telford's road, the suspension bridge over the Menai Strait and the building of a breakwater in the nineteenth century all contributed to the strategic significance of the town. Most recently the completion of the A55 across Anglesey brings a dual carriageway to the very gates of the ferry terminal. There are frequent sailings from here to Dublin and Dun Laoghaire, with the fastest crossing time being about 1¾ hours. Economic day trips for foot passengers are available from both operators. On the outskirts of Holyhead the landscape is dominated by Holyhead Mountain, capped by an iron-age fort. On the far side of the mountain, you can descend the cliffs by a series of staircases to reach South Stack lighthouse. Nearby is a seabird centre run by the RSPB. The cliffs provide nesting sites for many seabirds, especially guillemots, razorbills and kittiwakes. There is also a small colony of puffins.

Leaving Holyhead on the main road, we cross the Stanley Embankment and leave the A5 at Valley to join a pleasant route up the north-western coast. The road rarely touches the sea but there are splendid views back across Holyhead and the sound of sea birds is never far away. Again, the precise route of your bus will vary according to the service but the villages of Llanfachraeth and Llanfaethlu are served by most. All variations offer an insight into the island, with views of rocky outcrops and occasional sea views. The Anglesey coast path offers one way of exploring the rocky coastline and sections can be walked using the bus as a way of returning to your starting point. Anglesey is rich in prehistoric relics and remains. Many tribes, some going back 9,000 years have left evidence of human occupation, including burial chambers, hill forts and standing stones. One such standing stone is situated just south of Llanfaethlu, next to the main road.

Wylfa nuclear power station is passed some way to the left. There is a visitor centre here offering free admission and guided tours. Nearby Cemlyn Bay is another bird sanctuary. The bus soon drops down into **Cemaes Bay**, an attractive seaside village with a small harbour and pleasant cliff walks. Originally a fishing village, with herring being especially important, Cemaes became a thriving port in the eighteenth and nineteenth century. Limestone, marble, bricks, corn, coal and flour all passed through the harbour. There was also some shipbuilding here. Just up the coast, and within walking distance along the cliffs or a quiet lane, is Llanbadrig church, dedicated to St Patrick. Local legend claims that in the 5th century the young Patrick was washed up on Ynys Badrig (Middle Mouse Island), a mile or so out to sea. He was washed ashore and, having been spared, founded this church in thanksgiving. A short way further along the coast is Dinas Gynfor, another hill fort, and the most northerly point in Wales. **Bull Bay** is centred round a small harbour and a bay bordered with small rock pools. The coast here offers pleasant, airy walks with sea views northwards.

The slopes of **Parys Mountain** rise inland from Amlwch. The most productive copper mine in the world was once here. Mining can be traced to Roman times but it was the Napoleonic wars in the late eighteenth century that saw its hey day, with demand for guns and cannons. Up to 1500 men were employed at one stage. The inside of the mountain is virtually hollow and its exterior gives the impression of a lunar landscape. There are trails to explore this historic site, but be careful not to wander onto private land and some areas are dangerous. Indeed, there are still active plans to reopen the mine and to extract zinc and copper. The feasibility study has also identified deposits of lead, gold and silver.

Amlwch to Bangor

The town of **Amlwch** grew with the copper mining. It is said that there were once 60 pubs in the town and the vicar could claim £15 per year for smoke damage. A gap in the cliff was widened to create a port in the 1790s and can still be used by pleasure boats. Three miles east along the coast from Amlwch is Llaneilian church. The present fifteenth century building is built on the site of a church built a thousand years earlier in honour of St Eilian by Prince Caswallon Law Hir who had been cured of blindness.

The route from Amlwch traces the eastern coast of Anglesey and you can enjoy views across the sea towards the Great Orme near Llandudno. Passing below Parys mountain and the village of Penysarn, the route passes through undulating country, more wooded than on the west side of the island. Soon after the tidal defile of Traeth Dulas, you pass near the remains of **Din Llugwy**, a group of huts dating from the late Roman era. Near this is a Neolithic burial chamber and remains of a twelfth century chapel. Quite a collection. These lie about half a mile off the road to the east.

The bus leaves the main road to serve the coastal community of **Moelfre**, whose lifeboat has a remarkable history of lifesaving and rescues. In 1859 the Liverpool-bound Royal Charter sank off the coast of Anglesey during one of the fiercest storms of the century. The men of Moelfre formed a human chain to pluck anyone who came close enough from the sea. Despite this, 495 lives were lost. Today, the Seawatch Centre recounts this history and offers you the chance to watch local bird life and passing ships.

The proximity of camping and caravan sites indicates your approach to one of Anglesey's most popular family resorts, **Benllech**. Nearby **Red Wharf Bay** offers a huge expanse of intertidal mud and sand, about 25 sq km at low tide. This attracts a large number of wading birds. The salt marshes and sand dunes around the bay provide the environment for a variety of limestone plants.

The final leg of the journey veers inland through **Pentraeth**, ignoring a side turning to Beaumaris. Soon the Menai Straits come into view and you drop down to Menai Bridge. Just to the north of the town is Pili Palas butterfly, bird and minibeast centre. This offers a variety of tropical wildlife, including free flying butterflies. The bus returns to Bangor over Telford's suspension bridge.

Other trips

There is a range of other possible trips on Anglesey. From Bangor and Menai Bridge you can reach the historic port of **Beaumaris**. Edward I's last castle, together with moat, is open to visitors, as are the old gaol and courtroom. The south-western part of the island includes some excellent dune and forest scenery around **Newborough Warren**.

Route Information

Section	Bus No.	Operator	Weekday frequency	Sunday frequency	Jny Time (min)	Rover tickets
Bangor-Holyhead	4	Arriva Cymru	Every 30 min	No service	90	FPN RR TT
Holyhead-Amlwch	61	Lewis y Llan	Every 2 hours	4 journeys	60	FPN RR TT
Amlwch-Bangor	62	Arriva Cymru*	Every 30 min	5 journeys	60	RR FPN TT
Bangor-Beaumaris	53 57 58	Arriva / Lewis y Llan	Every 30 min	Every 2 hours	35	RR FPN TT
Bangor-Newborough-Llangefni	42	Arriva Cymru	Every 90 min	Every 90 min	80	RR FPN TT

Places to Visit

Bangor Cathedral   01248-370693
www.esgobaethbangordiocese.org

Marquess of Anglesey's Column,
Llanfairpwllgwyngyll   01248-714393

Oriel Ynys Môn, nr Llangefni   01248-724444
www.anglesey.gov.uk

South Stack Lighthouse

Ellin's Tower RSPB Seabird Centre, Holyhead
01407-764973
www.rspb.org.uk/cymru

Holyhead Maritime Museum   01407-769745

Wylfa Power Station, Cemaes Bay   01407-711400
www.bnfl.com

Amlwch Heritage Centre
amlwch.net/heritage-centre.asp

Moelfre Seawatch Centre   01248-410277
www.anglesey.gov.uk

Pili Palas Butterfly, Bird & Minibeast Palace,
Menai Bridge   01248-716518
www.pilipalas.co.uk

Beaumaris Castle   01248-810361
www.cadw.wales.gov.uk

Ideas for walking

A 125-mile coastal walk runs around Anglesey and Holy Island offering an enormous variety of coastal scenery from dunes to cliffs. It is possible to walk all sections using a bus route to facilitate outward or return journeys. A guidebook is now available from tourist information centres.

A series of Circular Walks leaflets is also available from Tourist Information Centres. One leaflet covers a four-mile walk from Bull Bay, which is passed on the Holyhead to Amlwch route.

Refreshments

Holyhead, Llangefni and Beaumaris have a variety of places to eat, as well as Bangor itself. You will find pubs serving food in many of the villages, including Bull Bay and Cemaes Bay.

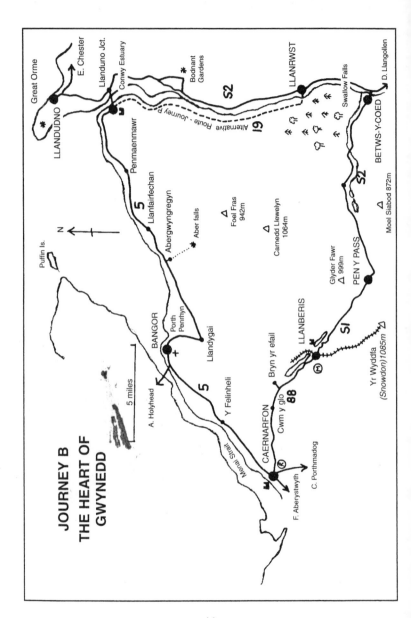

JOURNEY B
THE HEART OF GWYNEDD

46

Journey B: The Heart of Gwynedd

Llandudno – Betws-y-coed – Llanberis – Caernarfon – Llandudno

Climbing from sea level to the highest main road in Wales, this circuit embraces two great fortresses: the natural wilderness of Snowdon's mighty summit and the dramatic man-made walls of Caernarfon's castle. From the Victorian seaside resort of Llandudno, the route follows the east bank of the wide, tidal estuary of the river Conwy to Betws-y-coed. Wales' most popular inland resort nestles in the Gwydir Forest at the junction of several picturesque rivers. From here a steady climb up the wooded Llugwy valley leads to the summit of the road at Pen-y-pass, just three miles from the top of Snowdon. Descending through the slate town of Llanberis, you soon arrive in the historic walled town of Caernarfon on the coast. The return leg features spectacular cliff and coastal scenery backed by views of Anglesey and the Great Orme.

Llandudno to Llanberis
For more details about Llandudno see Journey D.

If you're lucky you might get an open-top Sherpa bus all the way from Llandudno to Snowdon. The Snowdon Sherpa is a network of bus routes that encircles Wales' highest and most popular mountain and offers easy and economic access to the mountain areas. The first section of this circuit makes use of the longest Sherpa route. In summer this runs from Llandudno all the way to Pen-y-pass, the nearest point by road to the summit of Snowdon. It is generally an open top bus, with a facility for carrying bicycles. Passing through the suburbs of

Llandudno the bus calls at Llandudno Junction railway station, a major stopping point on the London to Holyhead main line. It then joins the road heading south by the shores of the Conwy estuary.

The **Conwy Valley** has always been both an east-west barrier and a north-south communication route. Although this is a book about bus journeys, it would be churlish not to mention the Conwy Valley railway line, which accompanies the bus route as far as Betws-y-coed. This scenic route stretches for 28 miles from Llandudno to Blaenau Ffestiniog, climbing to 790 feet above sea level in the two-mile long Blaenau tunnel. Built between 1863 and 1879 it carried slate and later tourists. Nuclear traffic used an extension to Trawsfynydd from 1964 but that section of line is now disused. Red Rover bus tickets are valid on this line (but not on any other rail routes) so you could opt for a return trip to Betws using bus one way and train the other.

Passing through Glan Conwy, there are good views over the broad estuary, with Conwy castle on the far side. The bus route soon passes near **Bodnant Gardens** and some services divert from the main road to stop outside the gates. Cared for by the National Trust, Bodnant's world famous 800 acres are open to the public between March and October. A variety of formal and informal gardens offer a range of sights all year.

The river is never far away and is tidal for most of the way to Llanrwst. Look through the window and you have a good chance of seeing birds such as oystercatchers and herons feeding on the mud flats when the tide is out. Passing through the historic town of Llanrwst, the route continues to follow the main road with the hills of Gwydir Forest rising up on the west bank across the river. Shortly, you cross the river Conwy on Waterloo Bridge, built in 1815, year of its namesake battle before turning into Betws-y-coed. *An alternative route on the opposite side of the Conwy valley is described in Journey D.*

After calling at Betws railway station, our bus continues along the bustling main street, jammed with a combination of outdoor retailers, tourist memorabilia and cafes. **Betws-y-coed** is busy but nothing can take away its idyllic position commanding the confluence of several of Wales' most picturesque rivers. The Conwy, Lledr, and Llugwy emerge from the rocky heart of Snowdonia into the level, agricultural land of Dyffryn Conwy. The stout Victorian buildings, roofed in slate and overlooked by forested crags, make this an attractive place. Leaving Betws we ascend the valley of the Llugwy on a deceptively steep climb up the A5. In fact our route climbs almost continuously from Betws-y-coed, at only 20 metres above sea level, to Pen-y-pass, at an altitude of more than 350 metres. Some of the Sherpa buses have cycle pens, enticing cyclists to ride up on the bus, accompanying their bikes and then more or less freewheel back down.

A mile or so out of Betws, you pass the famous **Swallow Falls** on the right, where the river Llugwy tumbles over a series of rocky steps. The falls themselves are not easily visible from the bus but their position in a rocky gorge, surrounded by oak and beech woods is atmospheric. This is the most wooded part of Snowdonia and although much of the Gwydir Forest has been planted with conifers, many deciduous trees grace the scene as well. We stay with the Llugwy until we reach Capel Curig. On the right hand side, we pass Cobden's Hotel, which accommodates walkers, climbers, general tourists and... bats. Its rafters are home to the largest roost of pipistrelle bats in Wales, over 1500 in the summer months. Just past Capel Curig is the first panorama of the highest peaks of Snowdonia, mist permitting! This is the classic view of the Snowdon Horseshoe, with the graceful 1085 metre pyramid of Snowdon overseeing its supporting triumvirate of rocky peaks, Crib Goch, Crib y Ddysgl and Y Lliwedd. At the Pen y Gwryd Hotel the final ascent begins as the road climbs a narrow ledge towards the top of the Llanberis Pass. Over the precipice to the south there are views across Nant Gwynant. The pipes you can see carry water from Llyn Llydaw to Cwm Dyli power station, a hydroelectric scheme completed in 1906 to provide power for the local slate industry, and now one of the oldest operating power stations in the UK.

Pen-y-pass is the highest point of our route and terminus of this part of the journey. A youth hostel, café and bus interchange are all perched here, jostling for position with limited parking space and a plethora of boots and rucksacks. The two shortest direct routes up Snowdon, the Miners' Track and the Pyg Track, both start from this point, as does the classic Snowdon Horseshoe route which takes a dramatic course along the knife-edge ridge of Crib Goch.

You will normally need to change buses at Pen-y-pass. A frequent Sherpa service operates down the other side of the pass with the great shoulder of Crib Goch rising on the south side and the mighty mass of the Glyder range towering to the north side. The rocky glacial valley of Nant Peris opens up in front as height is lost. Llyn Peris comes into view with the great slate workings that brought prosperity to Llanberis gnawing deep into the slopes of Elidir Fawr. As you enter Llanberis you will notice the impressive round tower of **Dolbadarn Castle** overlooking the narrow isthmus between Llyn Peris and Llyn Padarn. Built at the time of Llywelyn the Great in the first part of the thirteenth century, the castle is believed to have been where Llywelyn the Last held Owain Goch captive for 22 years after his defeat in 1255. The castle has always been popular with artists and one look at its position and demeanour tells you why.

Llanberis to Caernarfon

Llanberis is built on slate. Although copper was mined here two hundred years ago, its topography, economy and culture are embedded in the hard slate from which the village was hewn. Slate was once shipped from here to many different countries in the world. The National Slate Museum of Wales is housed in the old quarry buildings, a short walk from the bus stop. The museum gives an authentic insight into the lives of slate workers and their families and includes a variety of exhibitions, demonstrations and videos as well as reconstructed furnished houses from different eras of history. The museum is situated on the edge of the 800-acre Padarn country park, which offers a variety of self-guided walks and includes several nature reserves and sites of special scientific interest. The old Dinorwig Quarry Hospital, hidden in the woods, is now open as a museum containing medical equipment from the nineteenth century. A former slate railway, now known as the Llanberis Lake Railway runs steam engines along a narrow gauge line by the shores of Llyn Padarn. Its station at Gilfach Ddu is adjacent to the Slate Museum.

Llanberis is built on slate but the mountain from which it was hewn has now been put to an alternative use, a cavernous home for Dinorwig Power Station. The main generating chamber, buried deep in the heart of Elidir Fawr, is large enough to hide any of Wales' cathedrals. Dinorwig is a pump storage power station, using surplus electricity to pump water from Llyn Peris up to Marchlyn Mawr, a lake high up in the mountains. When a surge of energy is needed at peak periods, the water is allowed to flow back down through tunnels in the mountains where turbines transform its power into electricity. It can start generating within 12 seconds and can produce enough power for the whole of Wales. Electric Mountain offers a range of presentations explaining the work, history and natural environment as well as providing minibus tours to the power station on the far side of Llyn Peris.

The famous Snowdon Mountain Railway climbs from the village to the summit of Snowdon. This is the only rack and pinion railway in the British Isles, carrying passengers up the 4.5 mile narrow gauge track at an incline of up to nearly 1 in 5. The engines push the carriages from behind as they make their way up the mountainside. Built in 1896, opinions vary on the etiquette of conquering Wales' highest mountain, said to be the resting place of King Arthur's knights, in such a way. But there are plenty of other ways up the mountain, and it would be churlish snobbery to deny the summit experience to all except those capable of toiling up the merciless scree from Bwlchysaethau or Llyn Llydaw.

The bus from Llanberis follows the southwestern shore of Llyn Padarn with more disused slate quarries rising up on the left. Most buses branch off the main road to serve communities such as Brynrefail and **Cwm-y-glo**. The latter name suggests that coal was mined in this valley, but it never was. The likely explanation for Cwm-y-glo's name ('coal valley' in Welsh) is that wood cut further up the valley was turned into charcoal here. In fact, boats came up the river to a small port where the school is now located. Passing through Llanrug, the mountain scenery gives way to more pastoral and agricultural terrain before you cross the Afon Seiont at Pont-rug. **Caernarfon** lies before you and the bus descends under the inner by-pass and on to the historic town's functional but sterile bus terminus at the back of a concrete shopping centre.

Caernarfon to Llandudno
Details about Caernarfon are included in Journey C.

There are frequent buses to Bangor and beyond and the route follows the main road. As you leave Caernarfon, there are clear views across to Anglesey across the narrows of the Menai Strait. A railway line ran to Caernarfon from Bangor until 1972. Escaping the mass closures in the Beeching era, it was one of a later collection of closures that seems now particularly foolish. Nevertheless, the track of the railway here provides the opportunity for a cycle track to enjoy the excellent views across the water. Soon the bus ignores the relatively recent by-pass to drop down into **Y Felinheli**. The small town was originally built as a port for shipping slate from the Dinorwig quarries we passed earlier in Llanberis. Its English name is Port Dinorwig. The slate was carried not along the coastal railway from Caernarfon, but across country on a steeply descending route directly from Llanrug and Llanberis. Today, sailing is a more common reason for using quayside facilities.

Between Y Felinheli and the outskirts of Bangor, the road passes the **Vaynol** estate on the left. A seven-mile long stone wall encloses A thousand acres of parkland. As well as the medieval Old Hall, there are many Tudor buildings including the chapel. King William III gave the estate to the English Assheton Smith family and the family began slate exploitation at the end of the eighteenth century. Today the estate is owned by the Welsh Assembly Government and the National Trust.

Passing a flyover link to the Britannia Bridge and Anglesey, the bus climbs up into the suburbs of Bangor, calling at Ysbyty Gwynedd on its way into the city. The station and main university buildings are passed before calling at Bangor's bus station, close to the city's ancient cathedral. *Details about Bangor are included in Journey A.*

The final section of route enjoys some spectacular coastal and mountain scenery. Leaving Bangor, you pass **Porth Penrhyn**, a harbour built to ship the slate from the Penrhyn quarries at Bethesda. The material was carried by railway. The track bed now provides the route for a cycleway into the hills. Penrhyn castle was built for the Pennant family from the profits of slate and sugar in the early nineteenth century. Today it is owned by the National Trust and open to the public. It houses a large variety of paintings and unusual artefacts such as a one-ton slate bed made for Queen Victoria.

Through Llandygai and the bus picks up the Expressway across the narrow coastal plain between the sea and the steep slopes of the Carneddau mountain range inland. It calls at **Abergwyngregyn**, from where you can walk up a charming wooded valley to the Aber falls, spectacular spouts of water pouring over a rocky ledge from the wild and remote Carneddau plateau. Seaward, the vast Lavan Sands are exposed at low tide. These intertidal flats are especially important to wintering oystercatchers and are home to 0.5% of the world's population.

There have been quarries at **Penmaenmawr** for over 5,000 years and tools produced here have been found all over Britain. Remains of the Neolithic axe factory can still be traced today. The present quarrying dates from the 1830s when stone was carried by tramway direct to a jetty. The quarry still produces stone today and is used for ballast, roads and tunnels, including the Mersey Tunnel. A legend tells of how a wicked sixth century prince, Helig, used to torture and murder local peasants for amusement. His sadism was abruptly terminated one night when a giant wave swept over his palace and drowned the prince and his courtiers. The imprisoned peasants escaped up the mountain. It is said that, at very low tide, the remains of the buildings destroyed can still be seen, while at high tide, a church bell can be heard ringing beneath the waves.

The coastal route is an engineering triumph. The Expressway was built in sections from the mid 1970s until the mid 1990s. This was one of the last sections to be completed and one of the most difficult. New tunnels drive the road through the seemingly impenetrable cliffs and road decks carry traffic on a narrow ledge between precipitous rock faces and the ocean. Beyond the cliffs lies the historic walled town of **Conwy**, itself now by-passed by means of a tunnel under the wide and tidal Conwy estuary. *More details about Conwy are included in Journey D.* The bus circumnavigates the walls before crossing the river by bridge. It is now just a short return trip to our starting point in Llandudno.

Route Information

Section	Bus No.	Operator	Weekday frequency	Sunday frequency	Jny Time (min)	Rover tickets
Llandudno-Pen-y-Pass	S2	Various	See note (1) below	See note (1) below	80	FPN RR SS TT
Pen-y-Pass-Llanberis	S1	KMP (Sherpa)	Every 30 min (Winter-hourly)	Every 30 min (Winter-hourly)	20	FPN RR SS TT
Llanberis-Caernarfon	9A 88	KMP	Every 30 min (2)	Hourly	35	RR FPN TT
Caernarfon-Llandudno	5 5X 9A	Arriva Cymru/ KMP	At least every 30 min	Hourly	95	RR FPN TT

Notes

(1) Services between Llandudno, Llanrwst, Betws-y-Coed and Pen-y-Pass:
Summer service (mid March to end October)
One morning journey runs daily (including Sundays) from Llandudno to Pen-y-Pass and there is a return evening run. Otherwise, catch bus 19 from Llandudno to Betws-y-Coed. From here Sherpa buses run to Pen-y-Pass every half hour until early evening.
Winter service (end October to mid March)
There are no direct services. Catch bus 19 from Llandudno to Betws-y-Coed. From here Sherpa buses run to Pen-y-Pass every hour during the daytime.

(2) Alternate services extend to Llandudno as service 9A.

Places to Visit

Bodnant Gardens   01492-650460
www.bodnantgarden.co.uk

Padarn Country Park, Llanberis   01286-870892

Welsh Slate Museum, Llanberis   01286-870630
www.mmgw.ac.uk

Electric Mountain, Llanberis 1286-870636
www.electricmountain.co.uk

Snowdon Mountain Railway, Llanberis 01286-870223
www.snowdonrailway.co.uk

Dolbadarn Castle, Llanberis www.cadw.wales.gov.uk

Caernarfon Castle (CADW) 01286-677617
www.cadw.wales.gov.uk

Segontium Roman Fort, Caernarfon (CADW)
01286-675625
www.cadw.wales.gov.uk

Bangor Cathedral 01248-370693
www.esgobaethbangordiocese.org

Penrhyn Castle, Bangor 01248-353084
www.nationaltrust.org.uk

Conwy Castle 01492-592358
www.cadw.wales.gov

Plas Mawr, Conwy 01492-580167
www.cadw.wales.gov

Aberconwy House, Conwy 01492-592246
ww.nationaltrust.org.uk

Butterfly Jungle, Conwy 01492-593149
www.conwy-butterfly.org.uk

Ideas for walking

Climbing Snowdon is a serious mountain expedition at any time of year. But for those properly equipped and experienced, the most direct routes lie from Pen-y-pass to the summit. The Miners' Track follows a broad track to Llyn Llydaw and Glaslyn before ascending very steeply up a scree path to the summit. The Pyg Track climbs more steadily towards the summit though it, too, concludes with a steep rocky section. The famous Snowdon Horseshoe starts from Pen-y-pass and climbs up on to the Snowdon ridge at Crib Goch. A knife-edge ridge follows to Crib y Ddysgl before leading on to Snowdon itself. The return route lies over Y Lliwedd. The Horseshoe is not an expedition to be taken lightly, nor at all in icy or windy weather.

Padarn Country Park in Llanberis offers a variety of waymarked routes in the woods and around Llyn Padarn.

Betws-y-coed also has some excellent walking and the Forestry Commission provides their usual high standard of waymarked walks in the surrounding Gwydir Forest. The Information centre near Betws rail station and bus terminus can give you more details.

Refreshments

All the towns en route offer a range of places to eat and general facilities. Betws-y-coed, Caernarfon, Llandudno and Llanberis are all major tourist centres and provide shops, takeaways and restaurants. Refreshments and toilets are also available at the bus exchange at Pen-y-pass.

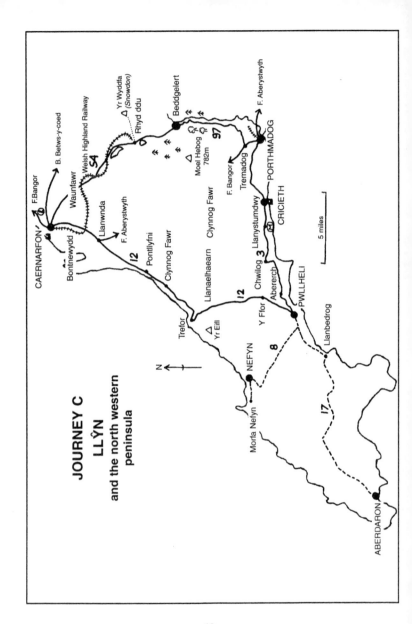

JOURNEY C
LLŶN
and the north western peninsula

Journey C: The Llŷn Peninsula

Caernarfon – Beddgelert – Porthmadog
– Pwllheli – Caernarfon

Trains once steamed across Snowdonia from Caernarfon and Porthmadog. Today the restored Welsh Highland Railway runs as far as the foot of Wales' highest mountain. The old line then snakes down the sylvan valley of the Glaslyn to reach the shores of Cardigan Bay at Porthmadog. This journey follows the course of the old tracks for most of its journey. To do so it makes use of the Snowdon Sherpa bus network that links communities and footpaths around the mountain. At Porthmadog we turn west to follow the coast of Cardigan Bay, with the distinctive silhouette of Cricieth Castle watching out across the sea. The return route from Pwllheli crosses Lleyn towards the wall of mountains that guard the peninsula's north coast. A narrow pass gives access to the coastline with spectacular views across the sea to Anglesey.

Caernarfon to Porthmadog
Caernarfon is an old regional centre. The early Celts had a hillfort above the estuary and later the Romans established their fort at Segontium to control north-western Wales. The Welsh princes held court there and when Edward I tried to colonise the country, Caernarfon became one of the priviliged imperial boroughs, guarded by a powerful castle. The great walls and towers of the castle were consciously designed to reflect the grandeur of Constantinople. The thirteenth century castle, built on the banks of the Menai Strait, dominates the town. Its once whitewashed walls would have glistened for miles around. The might of the castle and the town walls were

soon tested however when the Welsh, racially subdued and ethnically cleansed in their own country, rebelled time and time again. The most successful of the revolts was Owain Glyndŵr's long war of 1400-1415, when Caernarfon and the other castles were either captured or besieged and the colonists were virtually prisoners within their own walls while Glyndŵr went about his work of laying down the foundations of modern Wales. There is much still to see in the castle however, including the museum of the Royal Welch Fusiliers. The town's walls and narrow streets also merit exploration. There are pleasant walks on the other side of the Seiont, which can be crossed on a pedestrian suspension bridge.

The restored **Welsh Highland Railway** now runs as far as Rhyd-ddu, on the southern flank of Snowdon. One day it's hoped and planned that the whole route will be reopened. Its completion would offer the prospect of a circular rail tour including also the Ffestiniog Railway and Conwy Valley Line, with a connecting bus ride between Llandudno Junction and Caernarfon.

On the north side of the road out of Caernarfon lie the remains of the original Roman fort named **Segontium**. In 77AD northern Wales was conquered by Agricola and Segontium was one of a chain of forts built to secure the lands. It was built as a traditional Roman town and had access to tidal water in the river Seiont, after which it was named. The fort was occupied until 394, the last in Wales to be abandoned.

Crossing the Seiont and passing through Caeathro, the road wastes no time in heading for the hills. At Waunfawr the road follows the river Gwyrfai, and is now accompanied by the Welsh Highland Railway, which picked a more contoured route from Caernarfon's quayside. The road and railway wind along the watery valley floor, mountains soaring up to the sky. Snowdon Ranger Youth Hostel, on the banks of Llyn Cwellyn, is the start of a popular ascent of Snowdon. Just beyond, at Rhyd-ddu, the road approaches its summit and the present terminus of the restored railway. From here, a direct assault on Snowdon's peak can be made. Westward lies the slate stronghold of the Nantlle valley. Traversing the bleak and boggy watershed, the bus soon begins to descend Nant Colwyn alongside Beddgelert Forest.

You will need to change buses in **Beddgelert**. The village is barely more than a road junction for three mountain passes connecting Capel Curig, Porthmadog and Caernarfon. But its setting is idyllic, nestling in the wooded depths of the Glaslyn valley, a gurgling mountain stream tumbling over shattered rocks, soaring forests rising to the wild heights of Moel Hebog and Snowdon itself. Little wonder this is a honey pot for visitors. But perhaps the story of Gelert resonates with a peculiarly British sense of pathos and our island's inalienable obsession with domestic animals. Gelert was the faithful hound of Prince Llywelyn. While he was out at work hunting, he had arranged childcare with his dog, Gelert, who acted as nanny for the royal infant. One day returning from the chase, Llywelyn found Gelert covered in blood and no trace of the baby. In a rage he killed the dog. As Gelert let out his dying yelp, Llywelyn heard the cry of his infant son, safe and well. Alongside the child, he discovered the body of a wolf, slaughtered by the faithful hound. The story tells how Llywelyn never smiled again. The popularity of the touching story may owe more to the cynicism of nineteenth century commerce than to the integrity of Celtic mythology. In 1800 the landlord of Beddgelert's Royal Goat Hotel laid out Gelert's grave in its present place in the hope of attracting tourism to the remote valley. He certainly seems to have succeeded.

Beddgelert's mountainous location conceals its lowly elevation of only 40 metres above sea level. The sea once washed the rocks around **Aberglaslyn**, just two miles to the south. The road there is known as the Aberglaslyn Pass, contorting a route through rocky crags now conquered by a new menace, the rhododendron. Although the flowers are undoubtedly attractive, this oriental invader allows nothing else to grow and its prevalence is causing great concern. South of Aberglaslyn buses may take a variety of routes towards Porthmadog, some continuing on the main road, others diverting thorough Garreg, Rhyd or even Penrhyndeudraeth. The vast marshy floor of the Glaslyn valley was reclaimed from the sea by William Madocks' embankment at Porthmadog. The terminus of the Welsh Highland Railway marks the entry into Porthmadog. The southern stub travels a short way across the marsh in earnest of its aspiration to cross the mountains to Caernarfon. *(See Journey F for more about Porthmadog.)*

Porthmadog to Pwllheli

Although the route between Porthmadog and Pwllheli connects two coastal towns, much of the journey is a tantalisingly short way inland. It connects communities that were built a safe distance away from the wilder ravages of the coast. The bus passes north of the characteristic rocky profile of Moel-y-Gest and through the woods of Coed-y-Chwarel. The approach to **Cricieth** offers a clear view of the attractive seaside town, built around the castle, crowning a rocky headland facing out across Tremadog Bay.

Cricieth is a Welsh castle, the gatehouse built in the

thirteenth century by Llywelyn the Great. But Edward I in 1283 took the castle and he extended the fortifications, giving its present form. An exhibition traces Gerald of Wales' journey around the country to drum up support for the crusades. The main road through the town was a turnpike route, part of an unsuccessful attempt to draw Irish traffic to a new port at Porthdinllaen. On the eastern beach, the architect of Porthmeirion, Clough Williams-Ellis, designed the concrete Moranedd café.

A short distance west of Cricieth the twin rivers Dwyfor and Dwyfach are crossed. This is **Llanystumdwy**, home village of David Lloyd George (1863-1945) where his uncle brought him up. A museum tells the story of his life and political career as MP for Caernarfon and the last Liberal Prime Minister. The bus diverts through Chwilog and Abererch, as well as serving the holiday camp at Penychain. Views to the west encompass Abersoch and the Llanbedrog cliffs.

Pwllheli is in two distinct parts. The town, a busy, workaday shopping centre of no particular distinction and situated half a mile inland; and the sea front, approached by an attractive causeway across the harbour and marshlands. This is a holiday centre. Visitors crowd the streets and boats fill a marina. But it has not surrendered its cultural heart, which is firmly Welsh. And its pedigree is ancient too, the charter for the town's market dating back hundreds of years.

Pwllheli to Caernarfon

From Pwllheli, you can take a bus to Abersoch, centre for sailing. Beyond this, over the red cliffs of Llanbedrog, lies the very end of the Llŷn Peninsula at Aberdaron. **Bardsey Island** is just across the water from here. The 'island of a thousand saints', Ynys Enlli, is a powerful and evocative place of pilgrimage for the Celtic church. Day trips and longer stays can be arranged. Alternatively, a short bus ride across Llŷn brings you to **Nefyn** on the north coast. Remains of slate quarries and harbours are reminders of the industrial history of this region and today also offer outstanding coastal and cliff scenery.

This forty-five minute bus ride between Pwllheli and Caernarfon must be one of the most inspiring journeys in the country. The houses of Pwllheli are quickly left behind and a modest ascent gives a clear panorama across Tremadog Bay to Harlech and the Rhinog mountains. Through the village of Y Ffôr, there is a wilder feel to the country as you pass through the centre of the Llŷn peninsula and draw near to the looming peaks of the north coast. Around Llanaelhaearn, the mountains seem to close in all around. The three summits of Yr Eifl, incorrectly 'translated' as 'The Rivals', tower up to the west, capped by ancient iron-age forts. The craggy outcrops of Moel Penllechog rise up on the opposite side of the road. The road finds a way between these commanding sentinels to gain the north coast, opening up dramatic views across the water.

The bus leaves the main road to serve the cliff top community of Trefor, perched in the shadow of 'The Rivals' and boasting no fewer than three quiet beaches. Seals frequently come ashore here. From here, a look at the seaward side of Yr Eifl reveals the history of extensive quarrying, formerly a key industry on the north Llŷn coast. Between Trefor and Pontllyfni look across the water to Anglesey and Holyhead Mountain's distinctive outline at the tip of the island. Highlands dominate the inland vista as you pass through Clynnog but the coast is abandoned at Pontllyfni. Here the road takes a direct inland course towards Caernarfon leaving the marshes and sand dunes of Dinas Dinlle to the west. The Welsh Highland Railway joins us south of Bontnewydd where the river Gwyrfai crossed on the approach to the historic walled town of Caernarfon.

Route Information

Section	Bus No.	Operator	Weekday frequency	Sunday frequency	Jny Time (min)	Rover tickets
Caernarfon-Beddgelert	S4	KMP (Snowdon Sherpa)	Every 2 hrs	5 journeys	30	FPN RR TT
Beddgelert-Porthmadog	97	Express (Snowdon Sherpa)	Aprox hourly	3 journeys	20	SS FPN RR TT
Porthmadog-Pwllheli	3	Arriva/ Caelloi	Aprox _ hourly	6 journeys	35	RR FPN TT
Pwllheli-Caernarfon	12	Berwyn/ Clynnog &Trefor	Hourly	3 journeys	45	RR FPN TT
Pwllheli-Aberdaron	17	Arriva	8 journeys	No service	40	RR FPN TT
Pwllheli-Nefyn	8	Nefyn	Aprox hourly	6 journeys	15	RR FPN TT

Places to Visit

Caernarfon Castle   01286-677617
                                        www.cadw.wales.gov.uk

Segontium Roman Fort, Caernarfon   01286-675625
                                        www.cadw.wales.gov.uk

Welsh Highland Railway, Caernarfon or Porthmadog
                                               01286-677018
                                           www.festrail.co.uk

Sygun Copper Mine, Beddgelert   01766-510100
www.syguncoppermine.co.uk

Cricieth Castle   01766-522227
www.cadw.wales.gov.uk

Lloyd George Museum, Llanystumdwy   01766-522071

Bardsey Island Trust Office, Pwllheli   08458-112233
www.bardsey.org

Ideas for walking

There are relatively straightforward routes up to the summit of Snowdon from either Snowdon Ranger youth hostel or Rhyd-ddu. The Snowdon Ranger bus network enables you to vary the outward and return legs of your expedition, perhaps going down to Pen-y-pass on the road between Capel Curig and Llanberis. (See Bus Services in Scenic or Tourist Areas for more details.) But, be warned, Snowdon is to be taken very seriously. Proper equipment, precautions, navigation ability and experience are needed, whatever route you choose.

There are some excellent cliff and coastal walks from Aberdaron. The National Trust publishes some useful guides to these.

Refreshments

Fish and Chip shops abound in the seaside towns on the coast of Cardigan Bay. If you stop in Cricieth you could visit the Moranedd Café on the seafront, a listed building in 1930s style offering usual snacks and lunches, as well as buckets and spades.

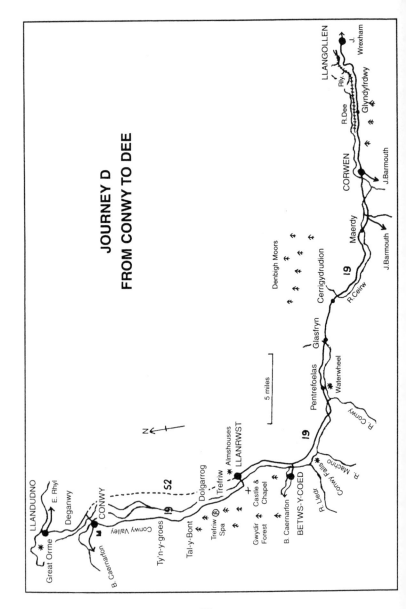

JOURNEY D
FROM CONWY TO DEE

LLANDUDNO

Great Orme

E. Rhyl

Deganwy

B. Caernarfon

CONWY

Conwy Valley

Ty'n-y-groes

S2

Dolgarrog

Tal-y-Bont

Trefriw Spa

Trefriw

Almshouses

LLANRWST

Gwydir Forest

Castle & Chapel

B. Caernarfon

BETWS-Y-COED

Conwy Falls

R. Lledr

R. Machno

R. Conwy

Waterwheel

Pentrefoelas

Glasfryn

Denbigh Moors

Cerrigydrudion

R. Cerw

Maerdy

J. Barmouth

J. Barmouth

CORWEN

R. Dee

Glyndyfrdwy

Rly.

LLANGOLLEN

J. Wrexham

N

5 miles

Journey D: From the Conwy to the Dee

Llandudno – Betws-y-coed – Llangollen

Over the past few years there has been a concerted attempt to create some strategic regional bus links throughout Wales. Bus X19 is an example of the strategy. For many years the service ran along the Conwy valley between Betws-y-coed, Llanrwst and Llandudno. Funding has now allowed an extension, several times a day, to Corwen and Llangollen. Previously buses along this section of the A5 were rare. You can never tell how long such an initiative, inevitably reliant on subsidy from local councils and the assembly, will last. So use it and enjoy it!

From Llandudno, route 19/X19 visits the ancient walled town of Conwy before following the west bank of the Conwy estuary through Dolgarrog and Trefriw. The wooded foothills of Snowdonia close in as you follow the road inland through Llanrwst to the tourist honey-pot of Betws-y-coed. From here the extended route X19 accompanies the livelier and younger river Conwy through a wooded gorge before reaching the more open and wild plateau around Pentrefoelas. The watershed passed, we descend gently into the catchment of the Dee, joining the river just before the historic town of Corwen. The wooded Vale of Llangollen completes our journey to the hometown of the international eisteddfod.

Llandudno
Llandudno was built as a seaside resort. It was carefully planned by Victorian architect Owen Williams under the direction of the Mostyn family, local landowners. The wide promenade fronted by elegant hotels and backed by the grandeur of the Great Orme appeals to a broad range of visitors today. The town itself also offers the best

shopping centre along the coast as well as good transport links by bus and rail. But the jewel in the crown is the Great Orme.

This limestone headland gives the town its own mountain, riddled with history and natural interest. The lower slopes host parks and gardens, while the summit plateau extends across heath, grassland and limestone outcrops. You can visit the summit by cable car or tramway in season. A toll road circumnavigates the headland. The summit complex and visitor centre offer a variety of attractions and refreshments but it is the limestone scenery and sea views, which make this place unique. Such is the panorama that the Great Orme was a semaphore station for shipping in to Liverpool. From the 1820s, messages could be carried to the port from Holyhead in just a few minutes. A little way below the summit, Great Orme Mines Visitor Centre offers an exploration of the mines, which date from the Bronze Age together with an imaginative audiovisual presentation. The prehistoric miners left hammers and bone tools behind as evidence of their activity.

Conwy

Leaving Llandudno through Deganwy, the bus soon crosses the estuary under the shadow of Conwy castle and next to Telford's original suspension bridge (1826) and Stephenson's tubular railway bridge (1848). The road bridge, more functional but less inspiring, dates from the 1950s.

The castle commands a rocky bastion overlooking the river while the magnificent Carneddau range provides an incomparable backdrop. Built between 1283 and 1289, the fortress was one of Edward I's imperial castles constructed because of the failure of his great armies to subdue the Welsh. The town itself was added as a fortified borough, an English privileged colony. The castle was captured by Owain Glyndŵr's men in 1401. Its town walls, largely intact, stretch for nearly a mile and included 22 towers, many of which still stand. You can walk on the parapet for most of the way and the prospect offers an excellent way of seeing the town and its surroundings. The castle can also be visited, courtesy of Cadw, which maintains it. Conwy has been relieved of much of its suffocating traffic by provision of a tunnel, which carries the A55 under the estuary. In the heart of the town, Plas Mawr, also in the care of Cadw, is one of the best preserved Elizabethan town houses in Britain. Once home of the Wynn family, the building includes a gatehouse and lookout tower.

The Conwy Valley

South of Conwy, bus 19 follows the west bank of the Conwy upstream. The mud and sand of the estuary always presented a barrier to invaders and travellers of all kinds. But the terrain represents life and nutrition to many species of waders. Look out of the window and the chances are you will see a heron. In 1925 **Dolgarrog** suffered a major disaster when Llyn Eigiau dam, high above the village, burst, and the torrent of water killed 16 people. The boulders and debris proved to be of such interest that the police had to erect roadblocks to keep onlookers away from relief workers.

There is evidence of Roman occupation around **Trefriw**. They probably made use of the Trefriw Wells Spa and had some mining interests in the area. The poet Taliesin was reputedly born on the shores of Llyn Geirionydd, in the forest above the town. In fiction, Trefriw is the birthplace of Brother Cadfael, the Welsh monk of Shrewsbury, in the medieval mysteries created by Ellis Peters and later televised. Today Trefriw Woollen Mills offer a variety of goods as well as a chance to observe the craft of weaving. Newly created Trefriw trails provide a chance to enjoy the forests and fields that surround the community.

Soon after Trefriw, you pass the entrance to the 16th century **Gwydir Castle**, ancestral home of the Wynn family, prominent landowners in northern Wales. Open to the public, there is an arch in the gardens built to celebrate the marriage of Charles I to his French wife. Immediately after the castle the road swings east to cross the Conwy by way of Llanrwst's seventeenth century bridge. For two centuries this was the only crossing of the river between the counties of Denbigh and Caernarfon.

Llanrwst's history dates back over 1,500 years. The parish church is dedicated to St Grwst, a sixth century missionary. Destroyed, along with the rest of the town in the Wars of the Roses, most of the present church dates from 1470. The almshouses were built in 1610 to house 12 local deserving poor and were used until 1976. They have recently been converted into a museum, opened by Lord Ellis Thomas in 2002. It is in the heart of Welsh speaking Gwynedd, and adheres to its motto 'Cymru, Lloegr a Llanrwst' (Wales, England and Llanrwst), in memory of more turbulent times when the town was in No Man Land's territory between the independent Welsh and the invading English forces. Twice during the 15th century, the town was burnt to the ground by English crown forces. Despite this the community failed in its attempt to gain a separate seat in the United Nations.

It is just four miles upstream to **Betws-y-coed**, reached by way of Telford's Waterloo Bridge, completed in 1815, the year of the battle whose name it bears. It bears an inscription explaining the connection. Betws-y-coed stands at the confluence of the Conwy, Machno, Lledr and Llugwy rivers. Much of it was built in the nineteenth century and it is today the most popular inland resort in the north. It has a marvellous setting and its topography provides opportunities for many forest and mountain walks and cycling. A small museum at the station offers a glimpse at railway history and the opportunity to ride on a miniature railway and tram. The Conwy Valley railway itself is a scenic journey in its own right. A Red Rover bus ticket includes travel on this line between Llandudno and Blaenau Ffestiniog.

Betws-y-coed to Llangollen

From here to the terminus our route lies along Telford's turnpike road built as a direct link from Holyhead and Ireland. It may not have the dramatic impact of the engineer's Menai crossing or Pontcysyllte aqueduct, but it is still something of a feat. The road winds up the wooded and rocky gorge of the upper reaches of the Conwy river, clinging precariously to the rocky ravine and twisting in concert with the natural contortions of the gully.

You can enjoy a closer look at the Conwy's adventurous tumble by admiring the **Conwy Falls**. The falls are in the grounds of the café and restaurant near the junction with the Penmachno road and can be visited for a modest charge. Self-guided walks take you through the woods and if you are very lucky you may see woodpeckers, dippers and even otters. To facilitate the migration of trout and salmon, a fish pass has been built comprising a series of 25 fish pools tunnelled under the rock. The restaurant building itself was designed by Clough Williams-Ellis, creator of Portmeirion and is painted pink as a reminder of this.

We lose the company of the Conwy just before Pentrefoelas and emerge in more open country with views of the Denbigh moors to the north and the wild uplands of the Migneint to the south. **Pentrefoelas** is easily missed, passed by cars and motorbikes hurtling towards the higher peaks of Snowdonia or the ice cream cones of Betws-y-coed. But pause here and you gain more of a real feel of the area, its culture and history. Pentrefoelas has a mill going back to the seventeenth century and still today a significant proportion of its population work in agriculture. One of its sons, Tomos Prys, fought Spanish ships in the Caribbean, seized a large quantity of tobacco and claimed to be the first person to smoke in the streets of London. He enjoyed fighting, poetry and music, an interesting combination.

The upper waters of the Merddwr lead towards **Cerrigydrudion**. There are wide views across the reedy valley to the hills beyond. George Borrow took this route in the opposite direction as he walked from Llangollen to Bangor. He records a sojourn at Cerrigydrudion, where he stayed at the Lion Inn. He tells us little of the place, but narrates a lengthy conversation with a doctor and the landlady about European culture. Past Cerrigydrudion, we soon join the waters of the Ceirw as they begin to descend from the plateau. This pleasant journey passes the sheepdog centre near Llangwm before crossing the river Dee just short of Corwen. The final leg of the route passes along the wooded and picturesque Vale of Llangollen through the historic village of Glyndyfrdwy, once home to Owain Glyndŵr. Today, you may catch a glimpse of a steam train on the preserved line that runs along the valley. *(More details of the route between Llangollen and Corwen can be found in Journey J.)*

Note - During Summer 2006, major road works near Cerrigydrudion caused alterations to this service. Check before travel.

Route Information

Section	Bus No.	Operator	Weekday frequency	Sunday frequency	Jny Time (min)	Rover tickets
Llandudno-Llangollen	X19	Arriva Cymru	4 journeys	2 journeys	130	FPN RR TT
Llandudno-Llanrwst	19	Arriva Cymru	Every 30 min	Hourly	55	FPN RR TT
Llandudno-Betws-y-Coed	19	Arriva Cymru	Hourly	Limited service	65	FPN RR TT

Places to Visit

Great Orme Tramway, Llandudno   01492-574234

Great Orme Cable Car, Llandudno   01492-877205

Great Orme Mines Visitor Centre, Llandudno
01492-870447
www.greatorme.freeserve.co.uk

Conwy Castle   01492-592358
www.cadw.wales.gov

Plas Mawr, Conwy   01492-580167
www.cadw.wales.gov

Aberconwy House, Conwy   01492-592246
www.nationaltrust.org.uk

Butterfly Jungle, Conwy

01492-593149
www.conwy-butterfly.org.uk

Trefriw Woollen Mills

01492-640462
www.t-w-m.co.uk

Gwydir Castle, Llanrwst

01492-641687
www.gwydir-castle.co.uk

Conwy Valley Railway Museum, Betws-y-coed

01492-610568

Conwy Falls, near Betws-y-coed

01690-710696
www.conwy-falls.co.uk

Plas Newydd, Llangollen

01978-861314
www.nationaltrust.org.uk

Llangollen Railway. Steam trains

01978-860979
www.llangollen-railway.co.uk

Llangollen Wharf. Canal cruises.

01978-860702
ww.horsedrawnboats.co.uk

Llangollen International Musical Eisteddfod

01978-862001
www.international-eisteddfod.co.uk

Ideas for walking

A stroll up the Great Orme will be rewarded by magnificent views. Follow the paths through Happy Valley near the pier.

'Trefriw Trails' is a network of routes that offer a variety of woodland and riverside paths of different lengths. A leaflet is available, or you can visit www.trefriwtrails.org.uk

Conwy Town Walls provide a grandstand view of the medieval walled town and its castle. If you have more energy, follow the North Wales Coast Path up the flank of Conwy Mountain to the west of the town.

Refreshments

A climb up the Great Orme will be rewarded not only with magnificent views, but also with a variety of facilities, including a café. Llanrwst, Betws-y-coed, Corwen and Llangollen have a range of cafes and shops. There is also a café in the Woollen Mill at Trefriw. If you fancy something sweeter, try stopping at the chocolate shop in Pentrefoelas.

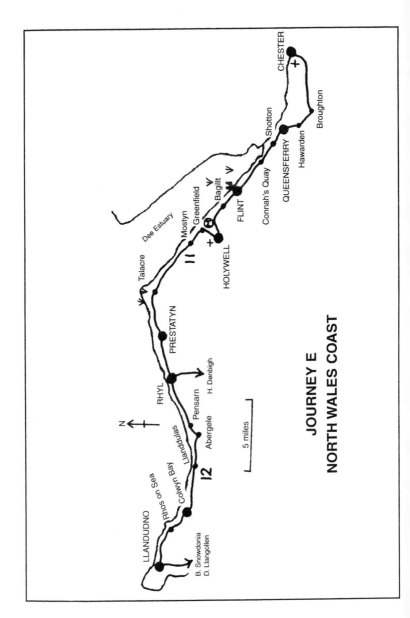

JOURNEY E
NORTH WALES COAST

CHESTER

Broughton

Shotton

QUEENSFERRY

Hawarden

Connah's Quay

FLINT

Bagillt

Greenfield

Mostyn

Dee Estuary

HOLYWELL

Talacre

PRESTATYN

RHYL

H. Denbigh

Pensarn

Abergele

I2

Llanddulas

Colwyn Bay

Rhos on Sea

LLANDUDNO

B. Snowdonia

D. Llangollen

N

5 miles

Journey E: The Northern Coast

Llandudno – Rhyl – Chester

East of Llandudno, the holiday coast stretches all the way to Point of Ayr, where it surrenders to the great estuary of the Dee. But there's far more to Wales' north-east than caravans and chip shops. The resorts themselves are quite distinctive, from the brash excesses of Rhyl to the gentler maturity of Colwyn Bay. Just scratch the surface to find a startling variety of natural history from rare plants on the foreshore at Pensarn to the unique habitat in the dunes and reed-beds of the Dee estuary. Venture a short distance inland and you'll discover one of the Seven Wonders of Wales, its holy spring that powered the might of the industrial revolution.

It's just a short hop along the promenade at **Llandudno** to the attractive crags of the Little Orme. Passing beneath these limestone outcrops, bus 12 then weaves through the pleasant but unexciting suburban areas of Penrhyn Bay and **Rhos-on-Sea**. Here, the harbour serves as a marina for small boats. St Trillo probably arrived in a small boat too, back in the days when the Celtic saints bobbed to and fro across the Irish Sea in coracles. The saint's chapel is tucked below the promenade, just north of the harbour.

A three-mile long curving promenade skirts the sandy bay, which gives **Colwyn Bay** its name and vocation. The expressway separating the town from the sea front was carefully constructed and has avoided turning Colwyn Bay into a kind of motorway service station. Wooded hills at Pwllycrochan above the town offer a variety of walks and also host the Welsh Mountain Zoo, founded in 1963. On a very clear evening, the views from the hills above the town stretch as far as the Coniston Fells in the English Lake District and Black Combe, north of Barrow-in-Furness.

East of Colwyn Bay, the road climbs past Eirias Park and through Old Colwyn to top the magnificent limestone cliffs at **Llanddulas**. The stone from the quarries here is shipped directly from piers at the base of the cliffs, carried there by cable cars. Inland, the river Dulas has carved a valley through the porous limestone bedrock, so providing a habitat for a variety of butterflies. Beyond Llanddulas, a long wall beside the road marks the boundary of the mock castle at Gwrych and you soon arrive in **Abergele**. This busy town is half a mile inland and the bus rejoins the coast by turning north to reach **Pensarn**, with its popular shingle beach.

A continuous series of caravan sites runs most of the way between Pensarn and Rhyl, supplemented with all you need for a British seaside holiday, amusement arcades, take-aways and launderettes. The arc-lit encampments of static caravans sandwiched between the incessant buzz of the main road and the frequent roar of express trains may not be everybody's idea of a dream holiday, but it is certainly popular with many. The sea is very close, as the residents of **Tywyn** remember too well. In February 1990 high tides overwhelmed the coastal defences and massive floods devastated many homes in the area. Much of the beach is a valuable natural asset and the shingle around Pensarn is a site of special scientific interest, home to locally rare plants such as Sea Kale. The North Wales Coast Path, doubling as a wonderfully level cycle way, drives its way between the caravans and the beach.

Caravans give way to bungalows in Kinmel Bay and the tidal estuary of the river Clwyd is crossed on the outskirts of Rhyl. The river was once a formidable obstacle to travellers and Edward I chose to guard the crossing at nearby Rhuddlan with a castle. Out to sea thirty wind turbines use natural energy to generate electricity in one of the country's largest wind farms.

Rhyl is the terminus of Arriva's number 12 bus and the stop is adjacent to the town's railway station. There's time to explore Rhyl, Wales' answer to Blackpool, whose tower lies just a few miles across Liverpool Bay and is visible from the hills above the town on a very clear day. There are miles of sandy beaches and plenty of entertainments for family holidays including the Sea Life Centre and the Sun Centre. Lasers light up the evening sky in season. The unremitting jangling of coins in gaming machines merges with the ubiquitous aroma of frying fat to offer the authentic atmosphere of a traditional British seaside town.

It's still absolutely flat as the bus heads east through Rhyl's suburbs. Between Rhyl and Prestatyn the bungalow is the predominant form of residential architecture, a reminder of the area's popularity among retired people. The road resolutely maintains its course along the coastal plain but the last gasp of the Clwydian Hills collapse down to the coastal plain directly behind Prestatyn, their limestone crags capped with thick woodland. Pleasant walks adorn these 'cliffs'. **Prestatyn** is a touch more genteel than Rhyl. The town is dissected by the Offa's Dyke Long Distance Path, which finishes at the Information Centre on the beach. According to various signs it is either 166, 177 or 182 miles to Chepstow, the southern terminus of the path. Whichever is accurate, it's a long but rewarding walk. The path weaves along the borders of Wales and England roughly following the line of the defensive earthwork built by

Offa in the eighth century, though there's no evidence of the dyke itself anywhere near Prestatyn. Prestatyn has a long history and there is some evidence of Roman occupation, such as a bathhouse, perhaps even a port.

East of Prestatyn green fields and trees replace the ribbon of human activity and development that has been our constant companion since Abergele. The bus passes through Gronant and a couple of miles further a roundabout gives access to Talacre and **Point of Ayr**. The dunes between Prestatyn and Point of Ayr are protected as a site of special scientific interest. The dunes themselves are home to some rare flora and fauna as well as providing habitats for many birds such as curlew, shelduck and oystercatcher. The RSPB has a reserve at Point of Ayr and Gronant dunes are the only breeding grounds for little terns in Wales. Apart from their natural interest, these sandy hills also provide important protection for coastal communities. Point of Ayr shares its natural riches with more contemporary human activity such as a natural gas terminal. One of the last deep coal mines in Wales was also situated here. There was once a lifeboat station alongside the lighthouse. Its last rescue took place on New Year's Day 1916 when the lives of 21 people were saved.

Between Point of Ayr and Greenfield, the seacoast is exchanged for the broad sands of the **Dee estuary**, with the Hilbre Islands and the Wirral coast on the far shore. Water from the mountains of Mid Wales finally merges with the salty waves of the Irish Sea in a vast expanse of sand and mud, washed by fast and powerful tides twice each day. Little wonder that this estuary, along with much of the coast here, is so valued for its bird life. The exact route along here varies, some buses deviating from the main road to serve communities now by-passed. Passing

Mostyn docks, a variety of old railway buildings come into view. Nearby a curious rusty ship was once an entertainment centre. Soon you arrive at **Greenfield**. All services turn inland here to climb up to Holywell. This mile-long ascent passes what must be one of the most intriguing combinations of sacred devotion and industrial activity anywhere in Wales.

The waters from the 'holy well' of St Winefride powered this hidden corner of the industrial revolution, leaving a fascinating collection of industrial and religious remains that could warrant a full day's expedition. The entire length of the stream from Holywell to the sea is only just over a mile, dropping a little over 60 metres. However, the original torrent gushed out of the rocks at the rate over 5,000 gallons a minute. Its flow was, until the early twentieth century, utterly reliable, and so provided a constant source of energy for a range of industrial use. The monks were the first to tame the force of the water to grind corn. The Cistercians, a popular order in Wales, built the abbey in 1132. It was closed during Henry VIII's first dissolution of monasteries in 1536 but the site is open and you can visit the substantial remains. A series of other mills made use of the torrent. The Parys Mine Company Site was once a copper works, built in 1787 by Thomas Williams. The name reflects his mineral interests near Amlwch in Anglesey and Williams earned the nickname of 'Copper King' for his energy and success. The mill manufactured rolled copper to protect the hulls of ships from parasites. Further up a range of other mills produced wire, copper sheeting, cotton and pottery. A branch railway line was built alongside the valley, ascending at up to 1 in 27, the steepest friction line in the UK. You can still follow its course along a footpath. These relics are all part of the **Greenfield Valley Heritage**

Park, which extends up hill from Basingwerk Abbey to the town of Holywell itself. The Greenfield Valley Museum is based in the Abbey's original farm and includes a Victorian schoolroom, a sixteenth century farmhouse and a variety of animals. The bus route runs up the road at the side, and you can enter or leave the park at a number of points in between.

Just below **Holywell** itself is the spring that inspired all this energy and much more drama besides. This is **St Winefride's Well**, one of the traditional 'Seven Wonders of Wales'. The well's legend dates from 660AD when Winefride, a young woman who felt called to the cloister, refused the advances of Caradog, son of a local chieftain. He attempted to rape her and then cut off her head with his sword. However, her uncle, St Beuno, performed a miracle by replacing her head and bringing her back to life beside the waters of the well. The earth swallowed up Caradog but Winefride lived as a nun for the following two decades. She was revered as a saint and her relics were eventually taken to Shrewsbury Abbey in the 12th century. Many stories of cures and healing originate from this time and the well has been a place of pilgrimage ever since. The original spring dried up nearly a hundred years ago, due to mining in nearby Halkyn Mountain, but a new source of water was found and diverted to the spring. Today pilgrims bathe in the waters, now housed in a shrine. Though the physical force of the water is diminished, spiritual power is still claimed. The spring is open to the public together with an interesting interpretative centre. There is historical evidence that Beuno and Winefride were historical figures. It would be foolish to dismiss the power of such a legend simply because of its anachronistic and unscientific genre. Though clouded by the mists of time and confused by the editing of later generations, the story may be based on some real events of heroism and bravery, offering inspiration today.

The bus descends from Holywell by one of two routes to rejoin the coast road through Bagillt to **Flint**. The town was built in haste as part of Edward I's drive to subdue Wales. So urgent was the construction that workers were brought from East Anglia and a ditch rather than a stone wall, provided the defences. Flint Castle was erected as part of this project and was the first of Edward's chain of castles, dating from 1277. The castle lies on the other side of the railway but is open to the public. The town itself is quickly passed, though the market place in the centre is an attractive focus. Just after Flint, the main road now crosses the Dee and the adjacent marshes on an elegant and dramatic suspension bridge. The bus still serves the urban areas the bridge was built to avoid. So our route continues through Connah's Quay to Shotton and Queensferry. These communities have always been a focus for industrial drive and energy. For many years **Shotton** steel works was a major employer. Household names like the frozen food group Iceland originated here. Lying on the banks of the Dee, just by the river's lowest crossing point, **Queensferry** has always been a crossroads, a genuine gateway to and from Wales. Roads from the north coast and Mid Wales converge with routes to Liverpool, Manchester and the English midlands. Once notorious for its queues, traffic today flows better, but still incessantly.

Before crossing to England, the bus route turns south climbing the short distance to **Hawarden**. The town's most famous son is the Victorian prime minister, WE Gladstone, who is buried in the parish church. He lived at Hawarden Castle, actually a castellated country mansion.

The original castle tops a mound in the parkland. Gladstone founded St Deiniol's Library in the town, today a study and retreat centre.

Hawarden overlooks the city of **Chester**, the great border stronghold. The bus now descends to the Cheshire plain through Broughton, home to an important segment of the British aerospace industry. You're still in Wales as you enter Saltney, effectively a suburb of Chester. In fact the bus crosses the border into England just a mile short of the historic centre of Chester.

Route Information

Section	Bus No.	Operator	Weekday frequency	Sunday frequency	Jny Time (min)	Rover tickets
Llandudno - Rhyl	12	Arriva Cymru	Every 10 min	Every 30 min	80	FPN TT
Rhyl - Holywell - Chester	11 11A	Arriva Cymru	Every 30 min	Every 2 hours	115	FPN TT

Places to Visit

Great Orme Tramway, Llandudno   01492-574234
www.greatormetramway.com

Great Orme Cable Car, Llandudno   01492-877205

Great Orme Mines Visitor Centre, Llandudno
01492-870447
www.greatormemines.info

Welsh Mountain Zoo, Colwyn Bay   01492-532938
www.welshmountainzoo.org

Sea Life Aquarium, Rhyl   01745-34466

Greenfield Valley Heritage Park, Holywell
> 01352-714172
> www.greenfieldvalley.com

St Winefride's Well, Holywell   01352-713054
> www.saintwinefrideswell.com

Ideas for walking
Walkers can also conveniently use the North Wales Cycle Path. The section between Pensarn and Colwyn Bay offers a five-mile level stroll on a good surface and the opportunity to return by bus.

Enjoy walks through the reserves and dunes around Point of Ayr. Alternatively you can walk up from Greenfield to Holywell through the Greenfield Heritage Park and return on the course of the old railway that ran steeply down from the town to the main line.

Refreshments
Of course, there is no shortage of fish and chip shops along much of the route. But there are plenty of other opportunities for refreshments. If you stop at Greenfield Heritage Park you could use the café there. Chester, Colwyn Bay, Rhyl, Prestatyn and Llandudno all offer the full range of facilities.

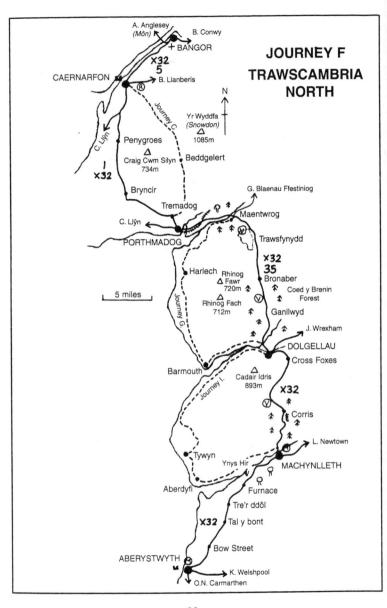

JOURNEY F
TRAWSCAMBRIA
NORTH

A. Anglesey (Môn)
B. Conwy
+ BANGOR
X32
5
CAERNARFON
B. Llanberis
®
Journey C
N
Yr Wyddfa (Snowdon) +
1085m
C. Llŷn
Penygroes
△ Craig Cwm Silyn 734m
Beddgelert
X32
1
Bryncir
G. Blaenau Ffestiniog
Tremadog
Maentwrog
C. Llŷn
Trawsfynydd
PORTHMADOG
X32
35
Harlech
Rhinog △ Fawr 720m
Bronaber
Coed y Brenin Forest
5 miles
△ Rhinog Fach 712m
Ganllwyd
J. Wrexham
DOLGELLAU
Barmouth
Cross Foxes
△ Cadair Idris 893m
X32
Journey I
V
Corris
L. Newtown
Tywyn
Ynys Hir
MACHYNLLETH
Aberdyfi
Furnace
Tre'r ddôl
X32
Tal y bont
Bow Street
ABERYSTWYTH
K. Welshpool
O.N. Carmarthen

Journey G

Journey F: Trawscambria North

Bangor – Caernarfon – Porthmadog – Dolgellau – Machynlleth – Aberystwyth

From the north's ancient ecclesiastical capital to the cultural and academic hub of mid Wales, the X32 'TrawsCambria' offers 90 inspiring miles of mountains, forests, estuaries and sea. Travelling through the historic fortress of Caernarfon, you skirt the fringe of Snowdonia to reach the northern edge of Cardigan Bay at Porthmadog. A climb up to desolate moorland leads to the wild forest of Coed y Brenin before the route descends to the Mawddach valley at Dolgellau. Another high-level traverse through the towering rocky scenery of the Cadair Idris massif leads to the slate valley of Corris. The river Dyfi, often seen as the geographical boundary between northern and southern Wales, is crossed to enter Machynlleth, for a few short months the capital of Wales. The Dyfi estuary, followed southwards, is a vital feeding station for many migrating birds.

The TrawsCambria service has a long and famous pedigree. For many years a single bus made a daily journey between northern and southern Wales as a practical and psychological thread uniting the famously disparate regions of the country. Few people actually made the whole journey from Bangor to Cardiff on the old TrawsCambria route 701 as it was neither fast nor convenient. In 2004 the service was split into two halves, dividing at Aberystwyth. The northern section runs from Bangor every two hours, covering the 90-mile journey in 3 and a half hours. This new service (and its southern twin from Aberystwyth to Carmarthen) (see Journey N) is aimed at middle-distance passengers to whom it offers a greatly improved facility.

Bangor to Porthmadog

Every bus in the north seems to call at Ysbyty Gwynedd, Bangor's hospital, and the X32 is no exception. Soon afterwards, the parade through Bangor's suburbia ends and the journey begins above the southern shores of the Menai Strait. *(For more on Bangor see Journey A)*. The first stop is at **Y Felinheli**. The village's English name, Port Dinorwic, is a reminder that a quay was built to ship slate. This was brought by tramway from the Dinorwic quarries around Bethesda. Approaching Caernarfon, the proximity of Anglesey belies the fierce currents and tidal races that endanger any crossing of the narrow Menai Strait.

Caernarfon breathes history. A Roman fort, Segontium, gives antiquity to its historic pedigree. The uniquely impressive Norman castle commands an unrivalled position on the waterfront, commemorating an era of violent struggle for the soul of Wales. The town walls, neglected and abused for centuries, were largely restored in the middle of the twentieth century and encompass a maze of narrow streets, giving this very Welsh town a cosmopolitan air. However, you will need to get off the bus to see most of this. The town's bus station, a series of bus shelters lined up next to a concrete multi-storey car park, is unlikely to be the subject of a listed building order. *(See Journey C for more about Caernarfon)*.

Morrison's supermarket greeted your entry into the town and its farewell is courtesy of Tesco. The wooded banks of the river Gwyrfai are soon crossed at Bontnewydd, while at Dinas you pass the restored line of the Welsh Highland Railway, which now runs as far as Rhyd Ddu at the southern foot of Snowdon. A different type of renewal has taken place on the disused track of the Caernarfon to Pwllheli railway, our companion for the next 10 miles or so. It has been resurfaced as a cycle route, Lôn Eifion. The railway formerly ran from Bangor to Afon-wen, near Pwllheli, where it joined the Cambrian Coast line. It was closed in the 1960s, though the section from Bangor to Caernarfon remained open until 1972.

The road passes the edge of an important slate quarrying area, upon which substantial villages like **Penygroes** were built. Slate outcrops on the surface in the Nantlle valley made this a key district for the industry. The valley still exhibits haunting and fascinating remains, inviting exploration at leisure.

The summit of the road at Graianog is 166 metres above sea level, amidst wild and open country. Past Bryn Cir and around the scattered village of Garndolbenmaen there is evidence of settlement deep into the mists of history. A steady descent off the plateau leads to the village of **Tremadog**. Snowdon Lodge, just outside the village, was the birthplace of Lawrence of Arabia.

Porthmadog is not an old town. Nor was it named after a Welsh prince. Its name is derived from William Alexander Madocks, a nineteenth century entrepreneur. Madocks built the embankment across the Traeth Mawr, now known as the 'Cob' as part of a grand scheme to carry a road from London to Dublin. The road was to terminate at Porthdinllaen, on the northern coast of the Lleyn peninsula, planned as a rival to Holyhead. A new town, Tremadog, was built just on the edge of the marshes with two main streets, London Street and Dublin Street, illustrating its purpose and importance. Although this dream was never fully realised, Madocks was also responsible for building the Ffestiniog Railway to carry slate from the mountains to the sea. The railway's workshops at Boston Lodge were named after the

Lincolnshire town for which he was the MP.

Porthmadog today is a busy crossroads and popular tourist hub. It is home not only to the Ffestiniog Railway but also to a short stub of the Welsh Highland Railway. Plans will link this to the more substantial section from Caernarfon that was passed further north.

Porthmadog to Dolgellau

Crossing Madocks' embankment alongside the Ffestiniog railway, the route passes through **Minffordd**, where the narrow gauge railway crosses the 'main line'. You pass close to **Portmeirion**, the Italianate village designed by Clough Williams Ellis in 1926 and famous as the set for the 1960s cult series 'The Prisoner'. **Penrhyndeudraeth**'s name signals its position between the two sands, Traeth Mawr and Traeth Bach and it's here that coastal waters are abandoned in favour of the valley of the river Dwyryd with steep wooded slopes rising up on either side. Below Tan y Bwlch, the bus pulls in at the **Oakeley Arms**, used as an interchange with buses between Harlech and Blaenau Ffestiniog *(See Journey G)*. The hotel is named after the Oakeley family, prominent local landowners, whose Tan y Bwlch estate extended to about 12,000 acres. Plas Tan y Bwlch is now a study centre.

A steady climb takes the road from sea level to a wild and desolate plateau around **Trawsfynydd**. Llyn Trawsfynydd's water was used to cool the reactors of Britain's only inland nuclear power station, though it is now being decommissioned. The village lies just off the main road and occupies a key site high up on the moors at an isolated and ancient cross roads. Its strategic position was not lost on the Romans. The name Trawsfynydd is derived from the Roman 'Trans Mons', across the mountains and a Roman fort and amphitheatre lie at Tomen y Mur just to the east. But this was also an ancient Bronze Age trade route between Wiltshire and Ireland and many standing stones and roundhouses speak of the millennia of human occupation of this isolated and remote settlement.

The high level section of road south of Trawsfynydd is fast and straight, with a grand vista of the **Rhinog** mountain range between the road and the coast. Between the stark profiles of Rhinog Fawr and Rhinog Fach lies the ancient pass of Bwlch Drws Ardudwy through the mountains to the fertile strip of land on the coast. South of Bronaber, the road descends through the Coed y Brenin Forest. A visitor centre interprets the geography and history of the area and the forest is popular with mountain bikers. Nature trails and a geological trail also help visitors to explore the mountainous terrain of the 'King's Wood'. At Ganllwyd, the Mawddach is followed down through the forest to Llanelltyd. Crossing the river, a fast road leads into Dolgellau.

Formerly the county town of Meirionydd, **Dolgellau** straddles the river Wnion. A maze of narrow streets focus around Eldon Square and the market hall. The town is a centre for rural and farming communities for a long way around and is also a tourist focus for the area. *(See Journey J for more on Dolgellau).*

Dolgellau to Machynlleth

From Dolgellau, the route climbs out of the Mawddach valley, twisting through pleasant wooded country to the isolated road junction at Cross Foxes. George Fox and John ap John travelled this road in 1657 and the area became a stronghold for Quakers. Quakers assert that a personal relationship with God, the 'light within', is the key to faith and life. They treat all people, including women, as equal, refuse to take oaths and have no clergy. They were often persecuted, especially after the restoration of Charles I in 1660. Many were imprisoned. Others emigrated to America after William Penn bought land there in 1681. The Welsh influence in the new state was evident. One university, Brynmawr, was named after the home of one of the émigrés, Rowland Ellis and today Pennsylvania remains an important focus for Quakers worldwide.

The pass of Craig y Llam leads through the mountains, with the crags of Cadair Idris towering to the north and the slopes of Mynydd Ceiswyn rising to the south. The striking scenery humbles a meagre trunk road, with heather clinging to mighty rock outcrops. Distant sheep pick their way through scree in their quest for patches of grass. A glacial valley carries the road down towards Tal-y-llyn but just before the lake it turns south to find a more direct route towards the Dyfi valley. A steep climb leads through oak and ash woods, conifers covering the higher slopes, and the road tops 200 metres above sea level before reaching Corris Uchaf. A long descent leads into the Dulas valley, a tributary of the Dyfi, as it twists through conifer plantations. The preserved **Corris** railway is a reminder that the valley was once one of the main centres for slate production in Wales. The Centre for Alternative Technology perches on the precipitous eastern slopes at Pantperthog. Eventually, the bus crosses the Dyfi, sometimes considered the geographical boundary between north and south Wales, and enters the town of Machynlleth.

Machynlleth to Aberystwyth
Machynlleth claims to have been the ancient capital of Wales, as indeed it was, but only for a few short months.

In 1404 Owain Glyndŵr held a parliament here and made it his base. You can still visit the site next to the Tourist Information Centre. *(See Journey L for more on Machynlleth)*. Passing the impressive town clock, TrawsCambria continues south, following the estuary of the Dyfi on its southern side. In a desperate attempt to avoid submission to the marsh, the road clings to the edge of its rocky curtilage. The salt marsh and dunes offer extensive intertidal habitats for wading birds such as dunlin, sanderling and ringed plover. The estuary is particularly important in providing a feeding station for birds migrating to and from breeding grounds in the north. The RSPB reserve at **Ynys Hir** offers the chance to explore this area. A huge waterwheel marks the site of the Dyfi furnace in the village of **Furnace**. Built in about 1755, it used water and charcoal to produce iron, but only for about 50 years. It was expensive to produce iron in this way, as an acre of trees produced only about a ton of the metal.

Emerging from the woods, the road discards the estuary and climbs to the village of Tre'r Taliesin, with good views across the low-lying marshes, Cors Fochno, towards the coast. **Tre Taliesin** is said to be the place where the legendary Welsh poet, Taliesin, is buried under a mound inside a circle of stones. A legend asserts that anyone who spends a whole night inside the circle will become either a poet or a madman. Taliesin is the focus of many ancient legends, among them that he was resident bard to King Arthur. Some of his poems and stories are believed to be accounts of Arthur's adventures, a mix of magic and myth. Poems and stories attributed to Taliesin indicate he was a bard who lived in the sixth century AD, though it is uncertain whether he was a single historical figure, or a single name given to a variety of Celtic writings. The earliest written examples of Taliesin's poetry date from 11th century manuscripts. Whatever the historicity of the authorship of these ancient tales, they are certainly authentic and formative expressions of ancient Welsh culture and that, rather than historical precision, is what gives power to myth.

A different spiritual opportunity invites visitors to **Tal-y-bont**, which boasts two adjacent pubs, the Black Lion and the White Lion. The route now lies through gentler agricultural country passing through Bow Street. The final section climbs a rise, entering **Aberystwyth** with a view across the town and Cardigan Bay. Descending Penglais Hill, the university, National Library of Wales and main hospital are passed and the longest bus route in Wales finishes in front of the town's Victorian railway station frontage (now a pub!) *(For more on Aberystwyth see Journey O).*

Route Information

Section	Bus No.	Operator	Weekday frequency	Sunday frequency	Jny Time	Rover tickets
Bangor-Aberystwyth	X32	Arriva / Express	Every 2 hours	2 journeys	3h 20m	FPN RR TT

NOTE - ADDITIONAL SERVICES

Most sections of the route have other services which, together with the X32, provide an hourly service during the daytime:
Service 28   between Aberystwyth and Machynlleth
Service 35   between Dolgellau and Oakeley Arms
Service 1   between Caernarfon and Oakeley Arms via Porthmadog

There are frequent buses between Bangor and Caernarfon

Places to Visit

Bangor Cathedral   01248-370693
www.esgobaethbangordiocese.org

Caernarfon Castle (CADW)   01286-677617
www.cadw.wales.gov.uk

Segontium Roman Fort, Caernarfon (CADW)
01286-675625
ww.cadw.wales.gov.uk

Welsh Highland Railway, Caernarfon   01286-677018
www.festrail.co.uk

Ffestiniog Railway, Porthmadog   01766-516006
www.festrail.co.uk

Welsh Highland Railway, Porthmadog   01766-513402
www.whr.co.uk

Porthmadog Maritime Museum   01766-513736

Portmeirion Village, Italianate village and shops
01766-770000
www.portmeirion-village.com

Coed y Brenin Visitor Centre, Ganllwyd   0845-604 0845
www.forestry.gov.uk

Corris Steam Railway, Corris   01654-761303
www.corris.co.uk

Centre for Alternative Technology, Machynlleth
01654-705950
www.cat.co.uk

Parliament House
Information Cen. & Owain Glyndŵr Centre, Machynlleth
01654-702827

Dyfi Furnace, Furnace 01654-781368
www.cadw.wales.gov.uk

RSPB Nature Reserve, Ynys Hir 01654-781265
www.rspb.org.uk

National Library of Wales, Aberystwyth 01970-632800
www.llgc.org.uk

Ceredigion Museum, Aberystwyth 01970-633088

Cliff Railway, Aberystwyth 01970-617642
www.aberystwythcliffrailway.co.uk

Ideas for walking
A series of self-guided trails help you to explore Coed y Brenin Forest from the visitor centre, details under Places to Visit.

Refreshments
Coed y Brenin visitor centre also has a café. You could choose to take a break at Porthmadog, Dolgellau or Machynlleth all of which have a selection of pubs and restaurants. Aberystwyth itself boasts a cosmopolitan range of eateries, some right on the sea front.

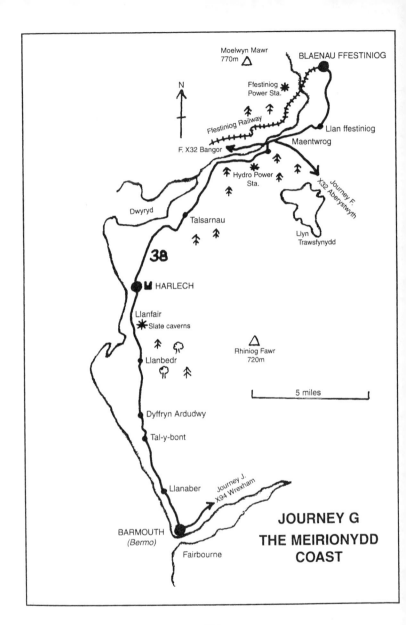

Moelwyn Mawr
770m △

BLAENAU FFESTINIOG

Ffestiniog
Power Sta.

N

Ffestiniog Railway

Llan ffestiniog

F. X32 Bangor

Maentwrog

Hydro Power
Sta.

Journey F.
X32 Aberystwyth

Dwyryd

Talsarnau

Llyn
Trawsfynydd

38

⚔ HARLECH

Llanfair
✴ Slate caverns

Rhiniog Fawr
720m △

Llanbedr

5 miles

Dyffryn Ardudwy

Tal-y-bont

Llanaber

Journey J.
X94 Wrexham

BARMOUTH
(Bermo)

Fairbourne

JOURNEY G
THE MEIRIONYDD
COAST

102

Journey G: The Meirionnydd Coast

Barmouth – Harlech – Blaenau Ffestiniog

The southern section of this route is a delightful coastal foray, juxtaposed between the mountains of the Harlech Dome and the wide seascape of Cardigan Bay. Harlech Castle stands sentinel above the coastal plain, guarding access to the interior of Meirionnydd. North of Harlech the route turns inland and follows the wooded estuary of the Dwyryd to the crossroads at Maentwrog, before climbing up in to the slate rich mountains around Blaenau Ffestiniog.

Barmouth to Harlech

Barmouth's location is its most precious and enviable asset. Sitting on a narrow shelf of land at the head of a golden beach, its houses cling to the bracken-clad hillside rising steeply behind the bustling main street. A busy harbour guards the entrance to the Mawddach estuary. A long sandy spit extends from the southern shore to within hailing distance of Barmouth pier. A passenger ferry crosses the narrows. From the far side you can catch a miniature steam train along the spit to the village of Fairbourne. The main line 'Cambrian coast' trains cross the Mawddach on the 113 trestles of the famous Barmouth viaduct. Built in 1860 and nearly 700 metres long, its elegant but vulnerable span frames the bay. A footpath, enjoyed by pedestrians for a small toll, accompanies the single-track railway.

An old legend holds that the rich land of Gwaelod lay out in Barmouth Bay, protected by a strong sea wall. The story explains the circumstances around the birth of Wales' oldest known poet, Taliesin. An irresponsible king neglected to ensure that his kingdom was properly defended against the sea. His son, Prince Elffin, saw the cataclysm coming and warned the people to move to higher land. Because of his action many were saved when the great flood came. But the land disappeared forever into Cardigan Bay and many others were drowned. A baby boy was rescued after being caught in a salmon trap. He grew up to become the mystical figure of Taliesin, the bard.

Space in Barmouth is at a premium. Never more so than on a damp bank holiday when the shops of Wolverhampton and Birmingham seem to have disgorged all their customers into Barmouth's branch of Woolworth's. Even on such a day you can flee the wet cagoules and sticky candyfloss in just seconds by climbing up the footpaths above the parish church on to the open hillside.

After a foray through a housing estate at the northern end of Barmouth, our route follows the coast along the main road. The shore is dotted with caravan sites and holiday accommodation most of the way to Harlech. But these developments don't impinge on the environment as grievously as on the north east coast. For one thing, the mighty hills of Ardudwy dwarf the barbeques and patio chairs that hug the coastal strip. For another, the majestic views across Cardigan Bay offer a perspective and proportion to human activity on the beach. It is a truly beautiful coastline.

Passing through the attractive villages of Tal-y-bont, Dyffryn Ardudwy and Llanbedr, you enjoy sea and mountain views along the route. From the coast, ancient mountain passes lead through the Rhinog Mountains and were routes of attack and defence. Just before Harlech, in the village of **Llanfair**, old slate caverns have been reopened to the public. They offer a glimpse of what was a vital industry in this part of Wales. The attraction is complemented today with a children's farm park and crazy golf course.

The sea once lapped at the foot of the rock on which **Harlech Castle** is built. Now the waters have receded but the dominant position of the fortress is still incontestable. Built by Edward I at the end of the fourteenth century, it was one of his 'iron ring' of castles designed to subdue the Welsh. Indeed, the castle hosted one of Owain Glyndŵr's parliaments in 1404. The fortifications rise straight out of the massive cliff face and command a view across the Irish Sea. From inland attackers would have had to contend with a huge gatehouse and ditch. The rousing song, 'Men of Harlech' was a response to a siege here during the Wars of the Roses.

Harlech is inextricably linked to the story of Branwen, daughter of Llŷr, mythical king of all Britons, recited in the Mabinogion. Outside the castle there is a sculpture by Ivor Roberts-Jones entitled 'The Two Kings' which commemorates the legend. Branwen, sister of Bendigeidfran, King of Britain, left the royal court in Harlech to marry the King of Ireland. Their son, the boy king Gwern was killed in the war that followed. In the sculpture, King Bendigeidfran bears the body of his nephew, Gwern. The inscription explains how it is a 'lament on the folly and carnage of war'. Apart from the castle, the town hosts a variety of cultural and artistic events. It is home to Theatr Ardudwy, Coleg Harlech and a variety of choirs and bands.

Harlech to Blaenau Ffestiniog

The bus winds its way down from the town and passes the station to follow a flat course across the dunes and coastal plain. The sea is never far away but soon it is apparent that our route is following the course of an estuary with the rocky wooded parapets of the Rhinog massif reaching up on the right. A toll road offers a shorter route to Porthmadog and the railway shares the crossing, but our route continues through increasingly wooded country on the south bank of the tidal Afon Dwyryd. Almost concealed on the right is **Maentwrog power station**. This is operated by British Nuclear Fuels but it is in fact, a hydroelectric station. Built in 1928, it can use up to 14 million gallons of water each hour.

Maentwrog itself gets its name from the giant Twrog, who is alleged to have thrown a huge stone down here. The rock sits in the graveyard of the parish church. The Oakeley family built the village to house workers on their Plas Tan y Bwlch estate. Their imposing mansion can be seen in the woods on the opposite side of the valley. To improve the view, an artificial meander was created in the river; it's still there today.

Most buses call at the interchange point at the **Oakeley Arms**. This enables connections with buses to and from Porthmadog, Caernarfon and Dolgellau. Many buses on route 38 finish here, in which case you will need to change buses to continue on to Blaenau Ffestiniog. This last section of the route continues to follow the Afon Dwyryd for a couple of miles before climbing up the side of the valley to reach Llan Ffestiniog. You may catch a glimpse of the Ffestiniog Railway on the opposite side of the valley as you climb up the hill.

The **Ffestiniog Railway** claims to be the oldest operating railway in the world. Today you can ride on steam trains between Blaenau Ffestiniog and Porthmadog throughout the year. An Act of Parliament incorporated the company in 1832 and the railway was built to carry slate down to the new harbour at Porthmadog. It is a continuous incline for most of the route and the system worked on gravity. The slate wagons were hauled back to Blaenau by horses. These animals then rode back down in 'dandy wagons' attached to the full slate trains, resting and feeding at the same time. In 1863 steam operation started and a year later passenger services were allowed. The line was abandoned in 1946 but a few years later a group of enthusiasts came together in an attempt to reopen it. The new passenger service started between Porthmadog and Tan y Bwlch in 1958 and was progressively extended until it reached Blaenau in 1982. The task was a huge challenge, not least because a pump storage power station scheme at Tanygrisiau flooded part of the old track bed to create its lower storage reservoir. A new route had to be devised and this involved creating a spiral loop at Dduallt. You can also visit the pump storage power station at Tanygrisiau, a mile from Blaenau. There are guided tours and a visitor centre.

The summit of the railway and the final terminus of route 38 is **Blaenau Ffestiniog**. Once the slate capital of the world, the old spoil heaps, now colonised by rhododendrons, encircle the town. One of the old caverns, Llechwedd, is a well-known tourist attraction and you can explore the inner recesses of this slate mine in the safety of the miners' tramway or a cliff railway. Llechwedd also offers audiovisual presentations on the history of slate here. Nearby Manod Quarry played a secret role in the preservation of the crown jewels and paintings by artists such as Rembrandt and Gainsborough during the Second World War. Churchill was advised to move many such works from the Tate and National Galleries in London and they were delivered to

Wales in vehicles disguised as chocolate vans. A cavern 200 feet high, deep in the mountain, was used as a national safe deposit box for the duration of the war and the caves were leased by the government as late as the 1980s.

Route Information

Section	Bus No.	Operator	Weekday frequency	Sunday frequency	Jny Time (min)	Rover tickets
Barmouth - Harlech-Oakeley Arms - Blaenau Ffestiniog**	38	Express Motors	Hourly	No service	65	FPN RR TT

NOTES
**Most services terminate at Oakeley Arms. Connections available to Blaenau Ffestiniog.

Places to Visit

Barmouth - Fairbourne Ferry   01341-250240

Fairbourne Railway   01341- 250240

Llanfair Slate Caverns and Children's Farm Park
01766-780247
www.llanfairslatecaverns.co.uk

Harlech Castle   01766-780552
www.cadw.wales.gov

Ffestiniog Railway   01766-512340
www.festrail.co.uk

Ffestiniog Power Station, Blaenau Ffestiniog
01766-830310
www.fhc.co.uk

Llechwedd Slate Caverns, Blaenau Ffestiniog
01766-830306
www.llechwedd.co.uk

Ideas for walking

This is excellent walking country, which offers many coastal and inland treks. Laurence Main's book, 'A Coast Walk in Meirionnydd' links stations (and bus stops) with walks between. If you want a shorter stroll, try the paths climbing up out of Barmouth for magnificent views.

Refreshments

After a visit to Harlech Castle, try calling at one of the teashops in Harlech town. Most of the coastal villages have good pubs offering a range of food.

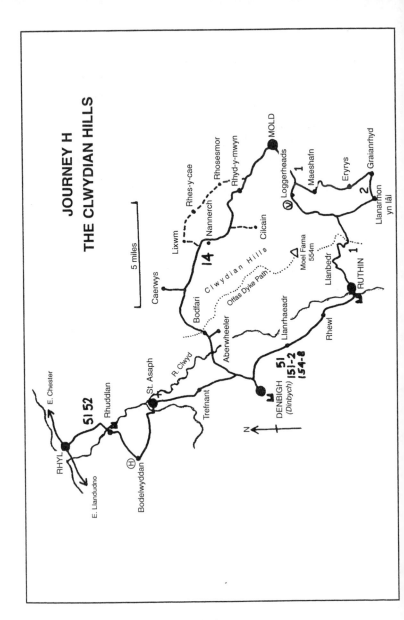

JOURNEY H
THE CLWYDIAN HILLS

5 miles

Journey H: The Clwydian Hills and The Vale of Clwyd

Rhyl – Denbigh – Ruthin – Mold – Denbigh – Rhyl

The Clwydian Hills rise steeply out of the lowlands of the Cheshire plain to mark the frontier between the lowlands of England and the uplands of Wales. Offa's Dyke long distance path runs along the length of the range, though the actual dyke probably ran further east through what is now the industrial area around Wrexham. The modern boundary also follows this lower land to the east of the range. The Clwydians are gentler and more rounded than the mountains of Snowdonia to the west. But the views from the ridge are stunning. From the highest point, Moel Famau, you can look across a wide swathe of northern England and clearly distinguish Liverpool's two cathedrals, Blackpool Tower and the Pennines. Westwards, your eye is drawn across the Denbigh moors to the serrated skyline of the Snowdon horseshoe.

The route starts by the sea in Rhyl, passing the medieval fortress of Rhuddlan and the cathedral city of St Asaph before reaching the historic county town of Denbigh. Beyond here the journey up the fertile Vale of Clwyd continues to Ruthin before turning east to cross the line of the Clwydian range. A gentler descent through limestone country brings us to Mold. The return route makes use of a charming, wooded low-level pass through the hills, once also used by the railway, to return to the Vale of Clwyd at Denbigh.

Rhyl to Denbigh

You either love or hate **Rhyl**. It is to northern Wales what Blackpool is to Lancashire. Fun fairs, arcades, candy floss and donuts jostle for position in a noisy and lively miasma of human activity, crowded with holidaying families from the neighbouring shires of Wales and England. Caravan sites spread along the coast either side of the town, any available space occupied by parasols and barbecues, any quiet place overwhelmed with the noise of booming music and the smell of charcoal. One of the assets of the northern coast of Wales is that if this is your idea of hell, you only have to travel one or two miles inland to be in a different world. Which is just what this tour does.

It's a relatively quick escape from Rhyl. Passing the supermarkets and light industry on the edge of the town, the flat coastal plain opens out ahead, backed by the hills of the Clwydian range. You soon arrive in **Rhuddlan**, dominated by the towers of its Norman castle. The fortress was built here because the river can be forded at this point, just below the tidal limit. It was the second of Edward I's colonial castles, built in the thirteenth century campaign to subdue the country. The river was diverted and canalised to allow access by ship and remains of the river gate can still be seen. The castle is a landmark for miles around and, nearby, remains of an earlier motte and bailey mound are still evident.

From Rhuddlan, the bus crosses the river Clwyd and continues across the coastal plain. Most services divert to serve Glan Clwyd General Hospital, some travel directly on the main road. Either way, the North Wales Expressway is reached just short of St Asaph. Most visitors swoop along the A55, passing the city in a matter of seconds and barely giving a glance to the cathedral set gracefully on a neck of land above the confluence of the Elwy and Clwyd rivers. Travelling by bus, you have the opportunity of a more intimate acquaintance.

Crossing the river Elwy on a seventeenth-century bridge, you climb up **St Asaph**'s High Street, passing the parish church on the left. The church is dedicated to St Kentigern who lived in exile here from 560 to 573, before returning to his native Scotland to become Bishop of Glasgow. In the church is the grave of Richard Jones, more commonly known as Dic Aberdaron. A linguistic genius, he was fluent in at least eight languages and his life's work was a Welsh-Greek-Hebrew dictionary, though it was never published. Dressed unusually and with long straggly hair, he travelled barefoot throughout northern Wales, carrying his books and a harp. Passing the seventeenth century Barrow almshouses, now converted into a restaurant, you soon reach the top of the hill, crowned by the smallest cathedral in Britain. It may be relatively modest in size but it's a pleasing, open building occupying an attractive situation. Outside is a memorial to Bishop William Morgan and the other translators of the first Welsh Bible in 1588.

After St Asaph the journey continues along the Vale of Clwyd through agricultural scenery. This is some of the most fertile land in Wales and the river flows wide and slow through fairly level countryside, carrying silt and sand on its sluggish trek towards the sea. But the hills are never far away. The eye is drawn to the Clwydian range marching along to the east, marked by the television mast at Moel y Parc. Through Trefnant, you soon reach the outskirts of Denbigh.

Denbigh to Ruthin

You approach **Denbigh**'s town centre by climbing Vale Street, accompanied by some elegant Georgian town houses, to reach the market place at the top. The medieval fortress town was a royal residence and stronghold of

Welsh princes before capture by Edward I in 1282. His castle still dominates the rocky mound on which the town is built and can be seen for many miles. The remains are cared for by Cadw and are open to the public. Denbigh has something of an air of tired dilapidation but it is a truly fascinating medieval town, complete with town walls and a range of historic and interesting buildings and alleys. Freed from honey-pot status and the associated deluge of tourists, you can enjoy exploring this historic town. As well as the castle you can see the Burgess Gate, the impressive medieval entrance to the old town. Nearby Leicester's Church was intended as a Protestant replacement for St Asaph Cathedral. It was connected to Robert, Earl of Leicester, Queen Elizabeth I's one time favourite, but it was never completed. Beatrix Potter and Samuel Johnson both had connections with the town.

Between Denbigh and Ruthin, the route continues to pass through the pleasant pastoral landscape of the Vale of Clwyd. The bus deviates through **Llanrhaeadr**, whose church is dedicated to St Dyfnog, a sixth century saint who was lured here by the healing waters of a nearby spring. There are many such wells in Celtic history. The church has some of the finest stained glass in Wales, including the Jesse window, depicting figures and symbols from Old and New Testament history. Mynydd Hiraethog, also known as the Denbigh Moors, rises ahead to the southwest. To the east, Jubilee Tower caps the Clwydian ridge on the 554m summit of Moel Fama. The road passes through Rhewl and you begin to see the houses of Ruthin ahead. We are now more clearly in upland country as hills increasingly close in around.

A legend says that King Arthur executed a rival lover in **Ruthin**. The Maen Huail stone in front of the Exmewe

Hall, now a bank, commemorates this gruesome tale. Better documented is another death in Ruthin, the execution of a Catholic priest in 1679. He was hung, drawn and quartered after a public execution in the town centre. The history is not all violent, though the men of Ruthin certainly worked up a thirst. When the population of the town was little more than 1,000 there were 10 pubs. St Peter's Square, the hilltop heart of the town, has a variety of interesting buildings. These include St Peter's Church, dating from 1284, and the Myddleton Arms, known as 'the eyes of Ruthin' because of its peculiar collection of dormer windows. The castle is now a hotel, but the old gaol is open to the public and offers an insight into the history of the town.

Ruthin to Mold

The Mold bus passes Ruthin School and soon begins the steep climb up the escarpment of the Clwydians. A series of sharp bends carry the road to the summit of the pass at 286m where Offa's Dyke footpath crosses the carriageway. It's a gentler descent on the other side, with the slopes of Moel Fama rising to the north and a lead-rich limestone plateau lying to the southeast. This plateau around Maeshafn and Eryrys was once a thriving lead mining area but now the villages lie in the heart of exceptional scenery with limestone pavements and beech woodlands. Some journeys extend to serve this area passing through Llanarmon yn Iâl, Graianrhyd and Maeshafn. The main route dips down to cross the river Alun at Loggerheads, a popular country park surrounded by woodlands with spectacular limestone cliffs towering above. Soon after **Loggerheads**, the town of Mold comes into view and, beyond it, a wider vista of the Cheshire plain.

Mold is a busy market town, the administrative and cultural centre of Flintshire. Its parish church was built by Henry Tudor's mother in thanksgiving for his victory at Bosworth Field in 1485. It occupies a fine location overlooking the main streets of the town. Theatre Clwyd draws audiences from a wide area. Mold has always occupied a strategic location as a gateway into Wales and it continues to exploit its position today with a variety of enterprises and industries located here.

Mold to Denbigh
From Mold our journey lies along a low level route back through the Clwydians. As far as Rhyd-y-mwyn, the road follows the valley of the river Alun before weaving a charming wooded passageway through the heart of the hills. Some journeys take a more northerly route around the side of Halkyn Mountain but this deviation rejoins the main route at Caerwys. Buses operate a circular route round the planned grid of streets in Caerwys before dropping back on to the main road. The tall television mast of Moel y Parc dominates the skyline at this point and it's not long before you emerge from the hills back into the Vale of Clwyd at Bodfari. From here three flat miles across the vale bring us back to Denbigh, its hill and castle standing out across the plain. If you're returning to Rhyl, catch the regular bus back, as on the outward route.

Other trips
Denbighshire County Council supports a network of routes known as Vale Rider and these provide other opportunities for travel.

Service 158 operates three times a day (Mon-Sat) between Denbigh, Ruthin, Llandegla and Wrexham.

Service 152 provides several journeys (Mon-Sat)

between Ruthin and Llangollen.

A one-day **Vale Rider** ticket is valid on all these routes, and on some other routes in inland Denbighshire, including the extensions to Llangollen and Wrexham.

Route Information

Section	Bus No.	Operator	Weekday frequency	Sunday frequency	Jny Time (min)	Rover tickets
Rhyl - St Asaph - Denbigh	51 52	Arriva Cymru	Every 20 min	Aprox hourly*	60	FPN VR TT
Denbigh - Ruthin	51 151 152 154 158	Variety of operators	Aprox hourly	Aprox every 2 hours*	25	FPN VR TT
Ruthin - Mold	1 1A 2	GHA	Every 1-2 hours	No service	30	FPN VR TT
Mold - Denbigh	14	GHA	Aprox hourly	No service	55	FPN VR TT

NOTES

* Evenings and Sundays - some through buses operate between Rhyl and Ruthin

Places to Visit

Sea Life Aquarium, Rhyl	01745-344660
Rhuddlan Castle	01745-590777 www.cadw.wales.gov.uk
St Asaph Cathedral	01745-583429
Denbigh Castle	www.cadw.wales.gov.uk
Ruthin Gaol and visitor centre	01824-708250

Loggerheads Country Park   01352-810614
                                www.loggerheads-northwales.co.uk

Ideas for Walking

Offa's Dyke long distance footpath crosses this tour twice, keeping to the highest ridge of the Clwydians for most of its length. It is possible to walk this section by leaving the Ruthin-Mold bus at Clwyd gate (the top of the hill) returning from Bodfari by bus 14 to Denbigh. This is over 10 miles of mountain country, so be prepared.

There are many shorter walks up and along the Clwydian range. Many start at Loggerheads Country Park. The visitors' centre has plenty of information and publicity.

Refreshments

There is also a café at Loggerheads Country Park. This circuit includes a number of towns offering a full range of attractions and eating places. Mold, Ruthin, St Asaph, Denbigh and Rhyl are all useful centres.

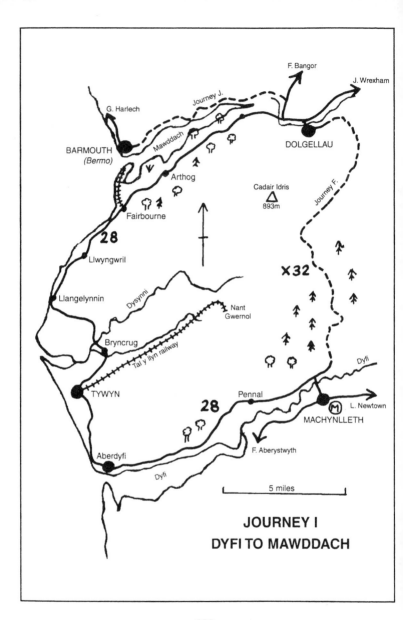

JOURNEY I
DYFI TO MAWDDACH

Journey I: From the Dyfi to the Mawddach

Machynlleth – Tywyn – Dolgellau

The direct route from Machynlleth to Dolgellau strikes out north to find a way through the mountains and forests. But this journey follows the western seaboard from the wide sandy expanse of the Dyfi estuary to the wooded shores of the Mawddach. On a good day, you can see the whole of Wales' western coast, from Strumble Head in Pembrokeshire to the holy island of Bardsey off the very tip of the Llŷn peninsula. A legend tells of bells ringing out from a lost city beneath the waves of Cardigan Bay. But you are probably more likely to hear a whistle than a bell, as you pass two narrow gauge steam railways. Not to speak of a classic survivor of railway engineering, the Barmouth Bridge.

Leaving Machynlleth you cross the Dyfi into Gwynedd and turn west to follow the northern bank of the river for a short way. Abandoning the water, the route climbs a little way up into the wooded hills that reach down to the estuary. By the time the village of Pennal is past and the road is reunited with the Dyfi the river has grown into a substantial tidal estuary. Across the sand lies the Ceredigion shore with the hills rising beyond. The road follows a narrow terrace, often carved out of the rock, just above the foreshore and close to the Cambrian Coast railway, which now accompanies the bus for much of the way. The estuary grows still wider and as you approach Aberdyfi a narrow finger of sand dunes stretches most of the way across the water from the southern shore. This is Ynys Las, a nature reserve and popular beach.

Sailing boats adorn the shore at **Aberdyfi**. Palm trees

proclaim its mild, southern facing location. Colourful cottages and boarding houses skirt the shoreline of this popular and attractive seaside town. The folk song, 'The Bells of Aberdyfi', speaks of a kingdom submerged under Cardigan Bay. Although the Welsh poet John Ceiriog Hughes wrote the lyrics in the 19th century, the legend dates back to the Middle Ages. King Gwyddno ruled a city, which was kept safe from the sea by a large dyke. However, one day a young maid left the sluice open and the city was overwhelmed by floodwater. The King survived but the city did not. According to the legend, local fishermen heard the muffled clanging of bells echoing from the depths of the sea.

The route now turns north to follow the coast and skirts an extensive network of sand dunes, colonised by a golf course. Outwardly, **Tywyn** is an unremarkable place. Its name simply refers to the sand dunes on which the town is built. But it's also the coastal terminus of the Tal-y-llyn railway. The line was opened in 1865 to carry slate from the Bryn Eglwys quarries near Abergynolwyn to the wharf at Tywyn. After a serious rock fall in the quarry, slate traffic ended. The line itself would surely have been finished but for the energy of some determined enthusiasts. The first railway preservation society in the world was formed in 1950 and worked hard to restore the line from its dilapidated condition. Such was its dereliction that a contemporary American commentator described it as a 'bit of ornamental scrollwork'. Today the line offers a scenic seven-mile journey along the Fathew valley as far as the wooded ravine of Nant Gwernol.

Beyond Tywyn the road loops north to avoid the marshy coastal floodplain, following the lush banks of the meandering Dysynni. The river is crossed just after the village of Bryncrug and the road then follows an undulating course back to the coast, with the Cadair Idris massif rising up inland. The coastal views are truly stunning. On a clear summer's evening with the sun in the west, you cannot but be moved by the sight of the whole of the Llŷn peninsula and Wales' holy island, Bardsey, off its western tip. The road clings to a ledge between the boulder-strewn slopes above and the waves below. This is a celebrated section of the coastal railway line. More than once landslips have caused accidents and a rock shelter is now in place further along on the descent to Fairbourne. A plethora of caravan sites confirms the popularity of the coast with holidaymakers as we arrive in Llwyngwril. Soon the Mawddach estuary glints ahead with the houses of **Barmouth** clinging to the hillside on the far shore. The wooden railway viaduct leads enticingly towards the town, a little over a mile away. A pedestrian walkway accompanies the track. But by road, it's a twenty-mile deviation to cross the wide and strongly tidal Mawddach.

There is another way to Barmouth. Arthur McDougall built the Fairbourne Railway in 1895 to convey building materials for the construction of Fairbourne village. It stretches for $2^{1}/_{2}$ miles from the 'main line' station to Penrhyn Point, a spit of sand that stretches across the Mawddach almost reaching into Barmouth harbour. A pedestrian ferry crosses the gap. A museum, nature centre and café add to the interest at the Fairbourne end, while the intermediate station has contrived the longest place name in the world, according to the Guinness Book of Records.

'Gorsafawddachaidraigodanheddogleddollonpenrhynareudraethceredigion' means 'the Mawddach station with its dragon's teeth on the northerly Penrhyn drive on the golden beach of Cardigan Bay.'

Our route turns inland after Fairbourne to follow the southern shore of the Mawddach estuary. This was also the line of a railway that ran across Wales to Dolgellau, Bala, Llangollen and Ruthin, where it joined the Chester to Shrewsbury line. It diverged from the Cambrian Coast at **Morfa Mawddach** station, otherwise known as Barmouth Junction, and the track is now a cycle route as far as Dolgellau. The triangular platform can still be seen, now home to a car park for a local nature reserve, the Arthog Bog. This is home to many plants, butterflies and birds, among them reed buntings and curlews. Above Arthog village, a charming path climbs beside the picturesque Arthog Waterfalls to reach a fascinating and historic plateau, unseen from the coast, but home to many prehistoric remains. Now the road climbs alongside the rocky slopes of Cadair Idris, sheltered by trees on these lower slopes. It returns to the estuary at **Penmaenpool**, once part of the Penmaen Uchaf estate. The toll bridge, built in 1879, cuts a few miles off the trek through Dolgellau. The RSPB reserve here unusually uses a disused signal box as a hide. The woods offer habitats to a variety of small birds, especially warblers. The tidal estuary provides feeding grounds for many waders, including oystercatchers, redshanks and water rails, and also for otters. It is now a short ride into Dolgellau and the road deserts the Mawddach to cross the river Wnion as the town is approached. It's not the quickest way from Machynlleth, but it's certainly a varied and memorable trip along the edge of Wales.

Route Information

Section	Bus No.	Operator	Weekday frequency	Sunday frequency	Jny Time (min)	Rover tickets
Machynlleth - Towyn - Dolgellau	28	Arriva Cymru	Aprox every 2 hours	3 journeys	90	FPN RR

NOTES
An excellent circular outing can be devised by combining this route with the direct service
from Dolgellau to Machynlleth via Corris (services X32/35). This is described in Journey F.

Places to Visit

Parliament House, Information Centre & Owain Glyndŵr Centre, Machynlleth   01654-702827

Tal-y-llyn Railway, Tywyn   01654-710472
www.talyllyn.co.uk

The Fairbourne and Barmouth Steam Railway
01341-250240
www.fairbournerailway.com

RSPB Reserve, Penmaenpool   01341-422071
www.rspb.org.uk

Ideas for Walking
The Tal-y-llyn Railway provides opportunities for walks from stations along its route, including paths from Nant Gwernol, station, nestling in woods at the top of the line.

The Mawddach Trail is a nine-mile cycle track and footpath skirting the Mawddach estuary between Morfa Mawddach and Dolgellau.

Refreshments
Refreshments and other facilities are available in Machynlleth, Aberdyfi, Tywyn and Dolgellau.

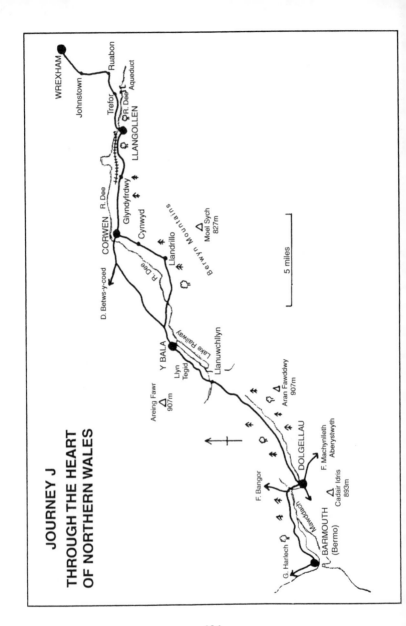

JOURNEY J
THROUGH THE HEART
OF NORTHERN WALES

WREXHAM
Johnstown
Ruabon
Trefor
R. Dee
Aqueduct
LLANGOLLEN
Glyndyfrdwy
CORWEN
R. Dee
Cynwyd
D. Betws-y-coed
R. Dee
Llandrillo
Berwyn mountains
Moel Sych
827m
Y BALA
Llyn Tegid
Lake Railway
Llanuwchllyn
Areing Fawr
907m
Aran Fawddwy
907m
DOLGELLAU
F. Machynlleth
Aberystwyth
F. Bangor
Mawddach
Cadair Idris
893m
BARMOUTH
(Bermo)
G. Harlech

5 miles

Journey J: Through the Heart of Northern Wales

Wrexham – Llangollen – Bala – Dolgellau – Barmouth

TrawsCambria service X94 takes you right through the heart of northern Wales, tracing the route of the old Cambrian railway to the coast. From Wrexham, the route climbs the Dee valley, one of the gateways into Wales. Passing through Llangollen and Corwen the route brings us to Bala. Following the shores of Wales' largest lake, the bus descends through wooded, rocky terrain to reach the market town of Dolgellau. Salt water soon comes into view as the bus hugs the shores of the Mawddach estuary, feeding ground to many wading birds.

Wrexham to Llangollen

Our route starts in the largest town in northern Wales, once the centre of a coal and iron district. **Wrexham** sits at the foot of a mineral-rich range of hills and at the gateway into the rugged hinterland of Wales. The remains of Wrexham's iron making past can be seen at Bersham Ironworks and at Minera Lead mine. Both these industrial sites are open to the public and interpret the industrial history of the district. The route from Wrexham lies through a series of industrial suburbs and villages. Soon after Ruabon, you pass through Cefn Mawr and near the large Monsanto chemical factory. But nearby is a memorial to an earlier industrial age. Telford's **Pont Cysyllte aqueduct**, built in 1805, carries the **Llangollen Canal** 40 metres over the Dee valley. You can enjoy an airy stroll across the towpath or take a boat trip. But, be warned! There is a parapet on only one side. The canal is a cul-de-sac off the Shropshire Union system and was part of a grand proposal for canal traffic. There are 46 miles and 21 locks between the intake at Horseshoe Falls near Llangollen and the Shropshire Union main line at Hurleston Junction near Crewe. Today the traffic consists of holidaymakers and you can see the brightly coloured narrow boats as the road and canal march jointly along the Vale of Llangollen.

Just after Trevor, the road crosses the line of Offa's Dyke long distance footpath. The 177-mile long path runs from Chepstow to Prestatyn. For most of its route it follows the line of King Offa's ninth century earthwork built to mark out his Mercian kingdom from Wales. The ditch and mound can be seen in many places, but not here. In fact, many experts believe the dyke itself went further east at this point, and that much of it has disappeared under the later industrial developments around Wrexham.

The route has now entered the mountains and the steep wooded slopes of the Vale of Llangollen beckon westward. **Castell Dinas Brân** stands sentinel above Llangollen. This hill top fortress was built by a local lord in the thirteenth century but was burnt down by the English in 1277. Today it is the crows, rather than medieval soldiers, that haunt the majestic hilltop ruins.

Llangollen itself guards the upper Dee valley. Here the river breaks out of the trough between the dramatic limestone escarpment of Eglwyseg to the north and the mass of the Berwyn Mountains to the south. The wooded valley invites visitors. Poet William Hazlitt called it 'this enchanted spot', and the ubiquitous George Borrow, Victorian traveller and writer, spent three weeks in the town on his journey around 'Wild Wales' in 1854. George Borrow's account of his epic walking tour is a classic.

Published in 1862, the book is a personal account of his experiences and encounters, as well as a descriptive narrative of the country and its people. Although he was from eastern England, Borrow had become fascinated with Welsh culture and had learned the language with the help of a Welsh groom and through reading poetry. He persuaded his wife and daughter to accompany him and on 1st August 1854 alighted from the train at Chester to walk across the border. His first sojourn was at Llangollen, where he stayed for nearly a month, exploring the Dee valley and surrounding area. He then set out on a tour of northern Wales, reaching Anglesey and Caernarfon before returning to Llangollen. After a shorter stay in the town, he walked through mid Wales by way of Bala, Machynlleth and Aberystwyth before continuing through Lampeter to Swansea. The final leg took him through Merthyr and Newport to leave the country at Chepstow in November. By any standards this was a long walk! You can still buy and read the unique guide of his travels.

Llangollen has always had its fair share of characters. Plas Newydd, a Tudor mansion on the southern outskirts of the town, was home to the celebrated 'Ladies of Llangollen' fifty years or so before Borrow's visit. After eloping from Ireland, they set up home in Llangollen. The house and grounds are now cared for by the National Trust. The town is perhaps best known for the annual International Musical Eisteddfod, held in July and centred on the pavilion at the west end of the town. Participants from over fifty countries converge on the Welsh language cultural festival, which began in 1946. The tradition of the eisteddfod is much older than this. The annual national eisteddfod started in 1789 in the Owain Glyndŵr tavern in nearby Corwen. It alternates between venues in the north and south of the country.

Llangollen to Bala

The bus follows the river as it continues along the A5, the route Thomas Telford carved through Wales in the nineteenth century to create a direct route to Ireland via Holyhead. The shapely ridge of Llantisilio rises up from the northern banks of the river. Soon after leaving the town you pass Berwyn, the first station out of Llangollen on the preserved railway line. The Llangollen railway runs between the town and Carrog, eight miles up the Dee valley. There is a planned extension to Corwen. Originally this was an important strategic route from Ruabon, near Wrexham right through to Barmouth, joining the Cambrian coastline at Morfa Mawddach. The through line was closed in the Beeching era but the eight miles of re-laid track serve steam and diesel trains which run for most of the year.

This is the country of Owain Glyndŵr, who had a home in the slate village of Glyndyfrdwy. Resentful at English plantagenet rule, and hungry through famine, the Welsh were ready for Glyndŵr's leadership. He challenged the authority of the English crown and gained extensive power and authority in large areas of Wales. The whole of Wales declared him Prince of Wales in the first Welsh parliment ever recorded, but by 1415 the English had re-established authority and Glyndŵr disappeared mysteriously into hiding. His dreams were realised by later generations and he is known as the 'father of modern Wales'. His grave is unknown. Glyndŵr's memory is kept alive in nearby Corwen, where a statue adorns the market place, as in many other locations in Wales. An Iron Age fort, Caer Drewyn, overlooks the town, which also hosted the first Urdd Eisteddfod in 1929.

From Corwen the bus takes one of two routes. Some journeys cross the river Dee and turn off the A5 at Druid to join the main road towards Bala. The road drives into the high pastures, with many views of the Berwyns and other mountains. Alternate journeys take the side road through Cynwyd and **Llandrillo**, following the Dee through the picturesque Vale of Edeyrnion. In the sixth century Trillo, son of a Breton missionary, established a church at Llandrillo. The churchyard contains an ancient yew, said to be one of the oldest in Wales. Its trunk is 4 metres in diameter and it is believed to be about 1500 years old. This, together with the circular shape of the churchyard, suggests a holy site a lot older than its Christian foundation.

Bala to Barmouth

Both routes arrive at **Bala**, built along its wide, bustling main street, with a range of shops and facilities. It lies at the head of the Dee valley, on the shores of Llyn Tegid, Wales' largest natural lake. The lake itself is host to a variety of water sports. Then town sits at the gateway of Snowdonia with splendid mountain views across the Arenig, Aran and Penllyn ranges. Steeped in Welsh culture and language, its history goes back to Roman times and beyond. The community has always been something of a focus for political and religious activity. One of the most famous stories is about Mary Jones' Bible. Mary Jones was born in 1784 in the village of Llanfihangel, near Cadair Idris. Bibles were then scarce in rural areas and, when she was 10, Mary started to save for her own. Aged 16, she had sufficient funds and heard that the Rev Thomas Charles, in Bala, was supplying them. Her only option was to walk the 25 miles, barefoot at times to save her soles. However, when she arrived the clergyman told her he had only one left and that was reserved. Seeing Mary's tears and moved by her great efforts, he gave her the Bible anyway and her story inspired him to make Bibles more available. In due course, what we know now as the Bible Society was founded for this purpose.

Another preserved railway makes use of the old track between Llangollen and the coast. The Bala Lake Railway runs steam trains between Bala and **Llanuwchllyn** on the eastern side of the lake, calling at Llangower. From Llanuwchllyn a minor road rises to the Pass of the Cross, a col between the Dee, Vyrnwy and Dyfi valleys, and the highest road pass in Wales at 545m above sea level.

From Llanuwchllyn, the road passes through remote mountainous country, but always with small settlements scattered along and around it. The watershed is soon passed and the route begins to drop down into the Mawddach valley, becoming increasingly twisty and wooded. Up to the right are the slopes of Aran Fawddwy, which gives birth to the Dyfi as well as the Mawddach. The Mawddach's route to the sea is much quicker than the course of the Dee. Like most west running rivers in Wales, it matures quickly, becoming broad and sedate as it enters Dolgellau. The bus pulls into the depot, which serves as a bus station and as an interchange for a number of long and short distance routes, including Traws Cambria services south to Aberystwyth, and north to Bangor.

Dolgellau is not a large town, with less than 3,000 inhabitants, but historically and geographically it occupies an important place. The town sits at a major junction of routes and at the lowest road crossing of the Mawddach, just below the massif of Cadair Idris. Owain Glyndŵr held his last parliament in the town in 1404. Its commercial importance grew with the woollen industry until the eighteenth century when mechanisation led to its decline. The nineteenth century gold rush was focused here and led to short lived speculation and activity. In religious history, the area has been associated with the rise of the Quakers and a local farm, Bryn Mawr, gave its name to a university in Pennsylvania.

From Dolgellau the bus follows the northern shores of the Mawddach, now tidal. Ruskin described this as the most beautiful journey in Britain. The intertidal sands are important feeding grounds for a variety of wading birds. On the opposite shore, following the course of the old railway is a cycle track and footpath, which continues to Morfa Mawddach. Barmouth's famous wooden railway viaduct is visible well ahead. As you enter Barmouth the waters of the Mawddach flow beneath the bridge to join the waves of the Irish Sea. You have completed a full traverse of Wales from border to coast on just one bus.

Route Information

Section	Bus No.	Operator	Weekday frequency	Sunday frequency	Jny Time	Rover tickets
Wrexham - Barmouth	X94*	Arriva Cymru	Aprox 2 hourly*	4 journeys	3 hours 20 min	FPN RR* TT

NOTES
*Additional services run between Wrexham and Llangollen to give at least a half hour frequency during the day. These are run by a number of operators (numbers 5,5A,X5,555). Red Rover tickets are only valid on the X94.

Places to Visit

Wrexham County Borough Museum   01978-317970
www.wrexham.gov.uk

| Plas Newydd, Llangollen | 01978-861314 |
| | www.nationaltrust.org.uk |

Llangollen Railway	01978-860979
	www.llangollen-railway.co.uk
Llangollen Wharf	01978-860702
	www.horsedrawnboats.co.uk

Llangollen International Musical Eisteddfod

01978-862001
www.international-eisteddfod.co.uk

| Bala Lake Railway | 01678-540666 |
| | www.bala-lake-railway.co.uk |

| Barmouth - Fairbourne Ferry | 01341-250240 |

| Fairbourne Railway | 01341- 250240 |

Ideas for Walking

From Llangollen enjoy a stroll along the towpath from Llangollen to the Horseshoe Falls (2 miles) or in the opposite direction towards Trefor. A steeper mile will take you to the top of Castell Dinas Bran with excellent views over the Dee Valley.

At Barmouth you could walk across the railway viaduct on the accompanying footpath for a small toll. A path and cycleway leads from the southern side of the viaduct at Morfa Mawddach along the estuary to Dolgellau.

Refreshments

Llangollen offers an excellent selection of hotels, cafes and restaurants. Refreshments are also available in Wrexham,

Corwen, Bala and Dolgellau. Barmouth has a range of places to eat, as well as a plethora of fast food outlets.

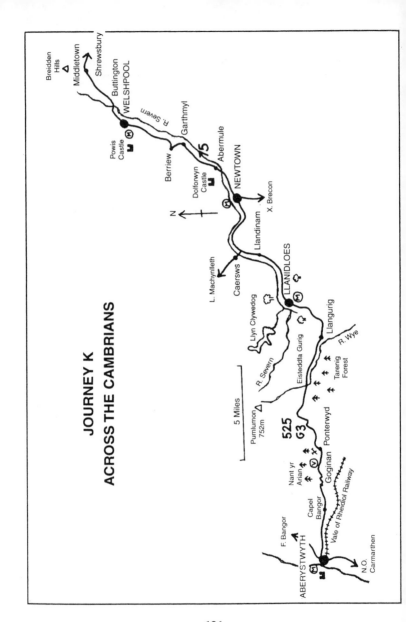

JOURNEY K
ACROSS THE CAMBRIANS

136

Journey K: Across the Cambrian Mountains

Shrewsbury – Welshpool – Newtown – Llanidloes – Aberystwyth

Perhaps it's Celtic romanticism, but a road through the mountains, especially westwards and sea-bound, always seems to have a spirit of adventure, purpose and anticipation. This is no exception, surely a classic traverse of Wales from east to west. Crossing the belt of the country at its narrowest point, our first bus takes us deep into the heart of mid Wales. From the historic border town of Shrewsbury, it pursues the wide valley of Britains's greatest river through Welshpool and Newtown to the market town of Llanidloes. The second part of the journey crosses the watershed into the dramatic wilderness of the upper Wye Valley, accompanying the energetic young river towards its source high in the Cambrian Mountains. Crossing the shoulder of Pumlumon there's a descent to Ponterwyd, crossing the Rheidol before a final ascent over Bwlch Nant-yr-Arian, haunt of the Red Kite.

Shrewsbury to Llanidloes

From Shrewsbury, the broad fertile valley of the Severn sweeps westward into the mountainous hinterland of Wales. The bus route follows the main road a mile or two south of the great river, undulating through pleasant agricultural country heading towards the dramatic rocky outline of the Breidden Hills. The road passes just below these distinctive forested crags as it crosses the border into Powys. Through villages of Middletown and Trewern, we emerge on the flood plain of the Severn, crossing the river and the line of Offa's Dyke at Buttington.

Welshpool lies ahead, guarding the broad route from the English midlands into the interior of Wales, its houses colonising the gentle wooded slopes that rise from the western edge of the Severn's wide flood plain. It is easy to see the town's strategic position as a gateway. Remains testify to Neolithic burial grounds in the fertile alluvium of the valley, and the Romans had an important burial site here too. According to legend, it was from this area that the Brythonic leader Caradog, or Caractacus, led his fight against the Romans, though it may have been from Llanymynech Hill, a few miles further north. In 1240, Welshpool was granted a borough charter and a thriving medieval town was built around Broad Street and High Street, where the bus stops.

Welshpool offers important insights into the history of transport. The Montgomery Canal arrived in the town in 1797 and its history, together with other aspects of the town's life, is recorded in the Powysland Museum and Montgomery Canal centre. The town's original name 'Pool' reflects its position on canal and river. It became Welshpool to avoid confusion with the English Poole, in Dorset. Some milestones still carry the old name. A narrow gauge steam railway operates on the 8-mile route from Welshpool to Llanfair Caereinion. The line was opened in 1903 and was never really successful as a passenger service, with trains running for less than 30 years, though a goods service continued until 1956. Restored in 1981, it now runs as a tourist attraction.

On the way out of the town, you pass the grounds of **Powis Castle** on the left. In the thirteenth century the original wooden castle was rebuilt in stone and it became the area's major stronghold through the middle ages. Today it is the seat of the Earl of Powis but is cared for by the National Trust and open to the public, together with its extensive seventeenth century gardens.

From Welshpool to Newtown our route follows the river upstream and southwestwards. The ridge of the Long Mountain strides along on the opposite side of the valley, while the main road sticks to the west bank of the Severn, sometimes accompanying the derelict but evocative Montgomery Canal. The bus deviates through the village of Berriew, crossing the river Rhiw as it tumbles down rocky rapids. Through Garthmyl, the bus crosses the Severn outside **Abermule** and branches off to serve this rapidly expanding village. Abermule was the scene of one of the worst railway accidents in British history on 26th January 1921. A collision between the Aberystwyth to Manchester express and a local stopping train resulted in the deaths of 17 people and injuries to many more. Strangely, the village's bus stop is used today as a driver changeover point. As you leave Abermule, notice the wooded ridge on the far side of the river. At the top of this ridge, though barely visible from the road, is **Dolforyn Castle**. Built by Llywelyn ap Gruffudd in 1273, it only had a short military life. The Prince of Wales built the castle in defiance of Edward I but it was captured by a Marcher baron, Roger Mortimer, just four year later after a siege lasting only two weeks.

A flurry of industrial estates, a golf course, a cemetery and Morrison's supermarket announce our arrival in **Newtown**, one of mid Wales' largest towns, though its population of little over 10,000 hardly ranks it as a sprawling metropolis. Evidence of one of Newtown's claims to fame can be seen in the large red brick mill on the left as you approach the town centre. This is the home of Britain's first ever mail order business, set up by the Pryce Jones family. *(For more details on Newtown see Journey L)*. Pulling out of Newtown Bus Station, the bus continues through the western suburbs of the town. Extensive housing estates were built here in the latter part of the twentieth century, part of a drive to develop Newtown as a pivotal community in the economy of mid Wales. Continuing upstream, with the river and railway line for company, bracken clad hills rise on either side of the valley.

At **Caersws** the valley opens out into a broad amphitheatre hosting the confluence of several rivers. Their valleys provide gateways through the mountains for several key historic routes. From the east, the road up the Severn valley from England; to the north-west up the Carno valley en route to the Dyfi estuary and Machynlleth *(Journey L)* and south westwards along the Severn to Llanidloes and over the watershed to the Wye Valley.

After turning into Caersws our bus takes the last of these routes, curving southwards as the road continues to follow the headwaters of the Severn. Ahead, the hills take on a starker, more dramatic outline with bracken climbing steep slopes to shapely summits ranging along the ridge towards one of the largest wind farms in the country at Waun Ddubarthog. The lush woodland and rich hedgerows of the valley provide a rich habitat for red campion and foxgloves in contrast with the lonely hills above. Through Llandinam and it's not far to the final destination of this bus in the market town of Llanidloes.

Llanidloes to Aberystwyth

The idyllic tranquillity of **Llanidloes** disguises its turbulent place in the industrial history of Britain. The wool industry was always important to the town, but in the depression of the 1830s its demise led to great poverty and the spread of Chartism and demands for economic

140

and political reform. On 30th April 1839, a riot at the Trewythen Arms led to the expulsion of the local forces of law and order. Chartists ruled the town for a week until troops arrived from Brecon. As in the south, the authorities, supported by rich and powerful vested interests, crushed the democratic ideals of the protestors. Over 100 people were punished, three being sent to the colonies, and the town remained under effective martial law for a year. What were the Chartists' treasonable demands? The most radical were secret ballots and universal (male) suffrage.

History is all around you in Llanidloes. In the seventh century, St Idloes laid the foundations of a church on the flat land of the Severn vale. The four main streets of the medieval borough meet by the unique market hall, built in about 1600 to replace an earlier building. The present hall has an open ground floor supported by pillars and is the only one of its kind in Wales today. John Wesley once preached here. Other timber-framed buildings are prevalent in the town and self-guided walks enable you to explore the history and architecture of the community.

Llanidloes is the first town on the Severn, which rises at 610 metres above sea level on the waterlogged wilderness of Pumlumon a few miles to the north-west. Britain's longest river, the Severn is 219 miles long and descends eastwards through Wales to the lower lying lands of the English midlands. Originally the river flowed north from Shrewsbury to what is now the Dee estuary, but geological upheaval around what is now the Ironbridge area forced the river south to its present course to the Bristol Channel. A few miles north of Llanidloes a 72-metre dam, the tallest concrete dam in Britain, has harnessed a tributary of the Severn, the Clywedog. Built in the 1960s, the dam was designed to control the water level by supplementing the flow in dry periods and retaining water at times of flood risk. The consequent lake, Llyn Clywedog, is scenically attractive and the remains of the old Bryn Tail lead mine in the shadow of the dam, can also be explored.

We leave the valley of the Severn at Llanidloes to follow a minor tributary, the Dulas. The bus turns and follows the old road through the attractive village of Cwm Belan. Weaving a route between steep, wooded hillsides, we climb up to the watershed between Severn and Wye. Crossing the summit of the road at Bwlch-y-Garreg, a new, wider vista opens up in front and, within a mile, you arrive by the banks of the Wye at Llangurig. The Wye and the Severn start and finish life together, rising just half a mile apart on the slopes of Pumlumon but following very different courses until their confluence at Chepstow. **Llangurig** is the first village on the Wye and also straddles an important road junction. We leave the A470 north-south trunk road here and turn west to drive a route through the Cambrian Mountains to the coast. Llangurig Parish Church was founded in the early sixth century. The present building dates from the fifteenth century but was extensively refurbished by Sir Gilbert Scott and boasts fine stained glass and woodwork.

There is an abrupt change of tone at Llangurig. Gone are the lush pastures of the Severn valley and the sylvan security of its woodland habitats. It's wild country now. The road from Llangurig to the coast is a classic pass through the mountains. No strenuous gradients or ungainly hairpin bends but a continual sense of space and wilderness, echoing to the call of the curlew and overlooked by the circling gaze of the red kite. The road from Llangurig climbs steadily, following the juvenile Wye, wriggling its rocky course along the bottom of the valley through rough meadow pasture. As you steadily gain height, the river gains energy, its clear water splashing hurriedly downstream through the bracken, a silvery thread forcing a stony passage from the highest mountains. On the south side, Tarenig Forest clings to the mountainsides and, at Pont Rhydgaled, the Wye is crossed and left in lonely isolation for its final three miles up to its marshy birthplace on the wild massif of Pumlumon. The road follows a tributary, the Afon Tarenig up the final ascent. The summit is reached at Eisteddfa Gurig where road crosses the shoulder of Pumlumon and begins to drop into the valley of the Rheidol on its journey to the west coast. It's a steep descent past the lonely hostelry of Dyffryn Castell to the village of **Ponterwyd**, where the Rheidol is crossed.

If you get a chance to spend some time in this area, you will be well rewarded. The Rheidol valley passes through excellent walking and mountain biking country. Upstream, the extensive Nant y Moch reservoir was built in 1961, while below the village, the river forces a passage through a gorge on its journey to Devil's Bridge a few miles south. This was silver and lead mining country. In the 1740s a mineral vein was discovered at **Llwyernog**, a mile or so up the Aberystwyth road. But the heyday of the mine was during the nineteenth century when a Cornish company ran it. Many Cornish miners moved to Ceredigion and a long association between the two Celtic cultures persisted. At the beginning of the twentieth century, the zenith had passed and many miners moved south to the coalfields. The history of mining is traced by the Llywernog Silver Lead Museum on the site of the old mine.

There were once 70 lead mines in north Ceredigion but it's timber that the land yields today. Soon after the mine and museum, the bus reaches the top of the hill and the **Bwlch Nant-yr-Arian** Forestry Centre. Apart from a wide variety of walking and cycling trails, the centre offers refreshments and a chance to see red kites. The red kite was a commonplace bird, even in British cities, until the sixteenth century. At that time laws were passed declaring the birds to be vermin and inaugurating two centuries of unparalleled persecution. By the end of the eighteenth century, the species had become extinct in England and Scotland. Kites maintained a slender claw-hold on existence in two mid Wales valleys alone. Thanks to conservation and legal protection, ultimate annihilation was evaded. There are now about three hundred breeding pairs in Wales. You will see the wide soaring wingspan of these magnificent raptors at many places, especially in the remote Cambrian Mountains. Nowhere will you see them to greater advantage than at Bwlch Nant-yr-Arian, where the birds are fed at 3 pm every day (2 pm during winter).

Crossing the brow of the hill, the end of the journey lies in sight at last, as you glimpse the glistening waters of Cardigan Bay some eight miles ahead. The bus now enjoys a long descent, twisting round the contours of the hills into the valley of Nant-yr-Arian and through Goginan and Capel Bangor, where the valley of the Rheidol is rejoined after its excursion through Devil's Bridge. The river has also been used to generate electricity at the hydroelectric power station in Cwm Rheidol. This makes good use of the river's rapid descent from the heights of Pumlumon to the sea. The Severn takes over 200 miles to drop this height and the Wye over 150, but the Rheidol's journey to the sea takes little more than 25 miles. You may also catch a glimpse of the Vale of Rheidol Railway as you approach Aberystwyth. Opened in 1902, this narrow gauge steam railway was originally built to serve the lead mines further up the valley. British Rail ran it right up until 1989. Steam trains run the 12-mile journey to Devil's Bridge along a spectacular wooded route along the southern side of the valley.

The historic village of Llanbadarn Fawr marks the outskirts of Aberystwyth and the road into the town passes between Parc-y-Llyn retail area and the main buildings of the university up to the right. The bus soon draws into its terminus, right next to the railway station. You have crossed Wales from east to west on what, for my money, is one of the best journeys through the heart of Cambrian wild country. *(For more details on Aberystwyth see Journey O)*.

Route Information

Section	Bus No.	Operator	Weekday frequency	Sunday frequency	Jny Time	Rover tickets
Shrewsbury - Welshpool - Newtown - Llanidloes	75	Arriva Midlands North	7 journeys - some change at Newtown	No service	2 hours	FPN
Llanidloes - Aberystwyth	525	Arriva Cymru	3 journeys	No service	1 hour 5 mins	FPN

!! Warning

Services may be reorganised on this corridor. Possibilities include dividing the Shrewsbury-Llanidloes service into two sections, separating at Welshpool. The Welshpool-Llanidloes section could be a candidate for the TrawsCambria network. Operators will probably change. Having said this, the route itself appears secure and the scenery will not change!

Places to Visit

Welshpool and Llanfair Light Railway   01938-810441
www.wllr.org.uk

Powysland Museum and Canal Centre, Welshpool
01938-554656
www.powys.gov.uk

Powis Castle, Welshpool   01938-551929
www.nationaltrust.org.uk

Robert Owen Memorial Museum, Newtown
01686-626345
www.robert-owen.midwales.com

WH Smith Museum, Newtown   01686-626280

Newtown Textile Museum   01686-622024

Llanidloes Social and Industrial History Museum
01686-413777
www.llanidloes.com

Llywernog Silver-Lead Mine, Ponterwyd   01970-890620
www.silverminetours.co.uk

Bwlch Nant-yr-Arian Visitor Centre, Ponterwyd
01970-890694
www.forestry.gov.uk/wales

Ideas for Walking
The Forestry Commission waymarks various walks from
Bwlch Nant-yr–Arian Visitor Centre. These include a

stroll around the small lakes to watch red kites feeding and longer distance routes into the surrounding forest and hills.

Refreshments
Llanidloes is a charming break point mid way along this route. The town has a number of cafes and pubs offering food and refreshments. If you stop at Bwlch Nant-yr-Arian Visitor Centre, you will find a café there.

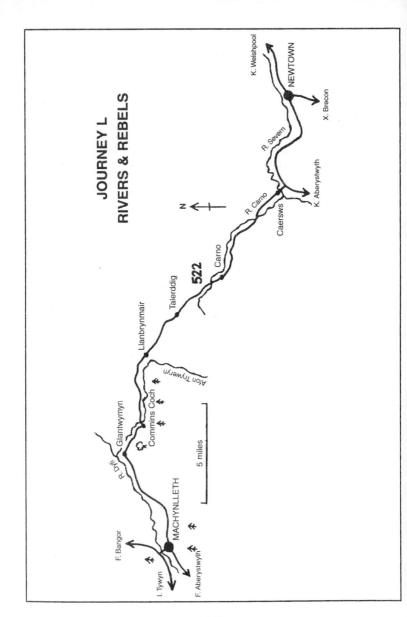

JOURNEY L
RIVERS & REBELS

N

NEWTOWN

K. Welshpool

X. Brecon

R. Severn

K. Aberystwyth

R. Carno

Caersws

Carno

522

Talerddig

Llanbrynmair

Afon Tryweryn

Glantwymyn

R. Dyfi

Commins Coch

5 miles

MACHYNLLETH

F. Bangor

I. Tywyn

F. Aberystwyth

148

Journey L: Rivers and Rebels

Newtown – Caersws – Carno – Machynlleth

Two different kinds of rebel have links with the beginning and end of this route. Robert Owen, born in Newtown, fought against Victorian industrial poverty and worked for a socialist utopia, though concentrating his efforts in central Scotland rather than mid Wales. Over 500 hundred years earlier, Owain Glyndŵr had struggled against the power of the English monarchy, leading a rebellion throughout Wales and making Machynlleth his capital for a few short years.

From Newtown, our journey lies along the Severn valley to Caersws, possibly the site of a decisive battle between Britons and Romans. Here the route turns northwest up the Carno Valley, home of Laura Ashley fashions. From the summit of the pass at Talerddig, a narrow passageway through the hills is shared by road and rail, descending to the Dyfi valley and on to Machynlleth.

Newtown spawned the first ever mail order business in the world, the first branch of WH Smith newsagents, and the most westerly outpost of Britain's canal network. The town's origins go back to 1279 when Roger de Montgomery used an older Welsh settlement as a basis for a planned 'new town'. Major expansion came in the nineteenth century with the arrival of the textile industry. Robert Owen was born here in 1771 and became a successful and wealthy Manchester mill owner. Owen became a leading inspiration for the socialist and cooperative movements, devoting much of his energy to developing an experimental community in New Lanark, marked by improved social and factory conditions and the provision of schooling. His life and work can be traced in the Robert Owen Museum. The first branch of WH Smith opened here in 1927. The shop still trades today, set out in the traditional counter style, rather more attractive and inviting than the ubiquitous plastic racks that dominate other stores. The first floor houses a museum telling the story of the firm.

The **Montgomery Canal** terminates at Newtown basin. As well as being at the western end of the navigation, it was also the highest point and so water had to be pumped from the Severn to supply the cut. The canal was part of an ambitious project to join the Dee and the Severn, but it never quite achieved its full objectives and was finally abandoned in 1944. Parts of the 'Monty' have now been restored and a 17-mile section around Welshpool is navigable.

Above Newtown, the hills either side of the Severn just begin to suggest a wilder aspect, with wood-framed farmhouses colonising the bracken-clad slopes. The valley opens out as the bus approaches Caersws, and the confluence of the Severn with two of its upper tributaries, the Carno and the Trannon, creates a broad amphitheatre in the heart of the mid Wales hills. The valley of the Carno carries the main A470 North-South Wales trunk, and the Cambrian main line railway, through the hills to Machynlleth. The route to Llanidloes and beyond continues in the company of the Severn.

Our bus turns in to **Caersws**, perambulating around the housing estate at the top end of the town. Caersws was probably a border stronghold of the Ordovices tribe who occupied much of central and northern Wales when the Romans arrived. In 51 AD, the Roman governor managed to force Caractacus, the Brythonic leader, into an open battle. This was probably fought near Caersws and resulted in the capture of the Brythonic Queen, though Caractacus himself fled further north. Evidence of Roman forts remains today. Eighteen hundred years later it was also chosen as a location for the workhouse to serve both Llanidloes and Newtown. Building started in 1838 in the face of fierce opposition by Chartists and others. The new building was the subject of sabotage while under construction and local people threw a government inspector's gig off the bridge when he came to the area to check on progress.

Leaving Caersws, our route follows the main road along the valley of the river **Carno**. Crossing the river at Pont Dol-goch, we soon pass through the village of Carno. Laura Ashley's fashion business relocated here in the 1970s. Born in Merthyr Tydfil in 1925, Laura Ashley set up the business with her husband in Kent, but soon moved to Powys. In the boom years other factories and outlets were set up in mid Wales and throughout the world but in recent years the quaint, flowery designs of clothes and home décor have struggled against cheaper, more modern designs. So in late 2004 the company announced it was relocating its operation to Newtown.

For most of this journey, the main road and bus route closely follow the railway. The Cambrian main line reaches its summit at Talerddig, over 200 metres above sea level, which is also a crossover on the single-track line. Beyond the summit, the line falls sharply at gradients up to 1 in 52, passing through a 30 metre deep rock cutting and then dropping through dramatic scenery on its journey to the Dyfi valley and Machynlleth. The road, too, finds the gap in the hills at the top of the Carno valley. It twists through the wooded gorge worn by the river Laen, through Dol-fach to the village of **Llanbryn-mair**, where the valley opens out. The settlement on the main road was called Wynnstay after the hotel situated here. The original village focused around the church, a mile or two up the Twymyn valley to the south. The Great Mound or Y Domen Fawr, on the outskirts of the village, is alleged to be the place where the poet prince, Owain Cyfeiliog, lived in a 'costly gilded castle.'

As we leave Llanbryn-mair, the Laen joins the Twymyn on the relentless descent to the sea, amidst the woods and flowers of the valley. At **Comins Coch**, the road imitates the contortions of the river as it twists a passage through the rock outcrops. The builders of the railway chose a profound cutting and series of bridges to negotiate the gorge. But, deep in the hills as we appear to be, we have almost reached the far side of Wales and another mile brings us in sight of the river Dyfi and the crossroads at **Glantwymyn**.

The final section of the route lies along the south side of the Dyfi. It's an undulating road with fine views along the valley. It veers away from the Dyfi to reach Penegroes, passing an old water mill, before entering **Machynlleth** along its main thoroughfare, Maengwyn Street. Half way along, on the right, is Parliament House. Owain Glyndŵr, the last rebel against the English throne, was crowned Prince of Wales near this site in 1404 and held a parliament here. The tourist information centre is housed in the building today. At the end of the street you will also notice the clock tower, built in 1874 to mark the coming of age of the eldest son of Viscount Londonderry. The Welsh language is strong in Machynlleth, as in most parts of north-western Wales. There is also a strong alternative 'green' culture in 'Mach' and the town has become a magnet for people seeking a more environmentally friendly lifestyle and pursuing a variety of related enterprises and activities. The Centre for Alternative

Technology is just three miles up the road towards Dolgellau.

Route Information

Section	Bus No.	Operator	Weekday frequency	Sunday frequency	Jny Time (min)	Rover tickets
Newtown - Machynlleth	522	Lloyd's Coaches	Four journeys	No service	75	FPN

Places to visit

Robert Owen Memorial Museum, Newtown

01686-626345

www.robert-owen.midwales.com

WH Smith Museum, Newtown   01686-626280

Newtown Textile Museum   01686-622024

Centre for Alternative Technology, Machynlleth

01654-705950

www.cat.co.uk

**Parliament House Information Cen. &
Owain Glyndŵr Centre**, Machynlleth   01654-702827

Ideas for Walking

The Glyndŵr Way is a 135-mile national trail between Knighton and Welshpool, looping around mid Wales. The westernmost point of the trail is at Machynlleth. Two sections of the path could be walked using the bus as a means of outward or return transport. Llanbryn-mair to Glantwymyn is a 6.5-mile stretch through the hills north of the main road. Glantwymyn to Machynlleth involves an 8.5-mile walk through country south of the Dyfi valley.

Refreshments
The towns at either end of this route have a selection of cafes, pubs and restaurants.

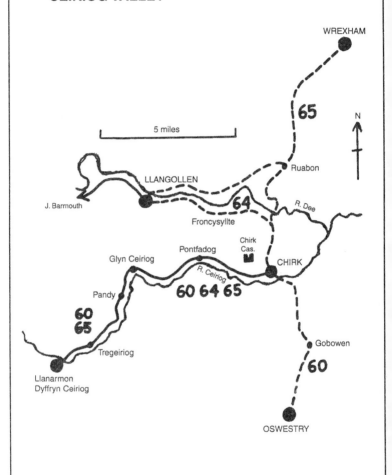

JOURNEY M
CEIRIOG VALLEY

WREXHAM

65

N

5 miles

LLANGOLLEN

J. Barmouth

64

R. Dee

Froncysyllte

Chirk Cas.

Pontfadog

Glyn Ceiriog

CHIRK

R. Ceiriog

Pandy

60 64 65

60
65

Tregeiriog

Gobowen

60

Llanarmon
Dyffryn Ceiriog

OSWESTRY

Journey M: The Ceiriog Valley

Chirk – Llanarmon Dyffryn Ceiriog

A series of valleys carry the rivers and streams of Wales eastwards into the English lowlands. These routes offer gateways into the mountains and have been used for centuries by travellers, drovers and armies. One such river has its source on the high slopes of the Berwyn. The Ceiriog forges a narrow course through Llanarmon and Glyn Ceiriog, forming the border with England for the last few miles before its confluence with the Dee near Chirk. Its waters eventually flow through Chester and into the Irish Sea.

The route up the Ceiriog Valley offers a short but scenic journey through a delightful valley and the opportunity to explore the natural environment and history of this part of north-east Wales.

We begin our journey in Chirk. However, buses actually start at Wrexham, Llangollen or Oswestry, so there is a range of possibilities for travel. (See Route Information). All Ceiriog Valley buses serve Chirk railway station and this interchange also offers opportunity to arrange a day out using the regular train service on the Chester - Shrewsbury line.

Chirk is positioned exactly on the border. Telford's main road, now known as the A5, enters both Wales and Chirk as it crosses the Ceiriog below the town. Chirk was given a charter in 1324 and the parish church dates from Norman times. In the eighteenth and nineteenth centuries, the development of industries such as coal mining needed transport. Telford's Llangollen Canal, part of the Shropshire Union network, was opened and an aqueduct built across the Ceiriog Valley in 1801. The railway came in 1852 and it too needed a viaduct to cross the deep Ceiriog valley. These structures now stand side by side and can be viewed well from the road up the valley.

After calling at the station, the bus route and road follow the northern bank of the Ceiriog through the trees. Small fields in the bottom of the valley give way to steeply rising wooded slopes either side of the river, with white painted houses dotted over the hillsides. Passing the trout farm and shop, the line of Offa's Dyke is soon crossed at Bronygarth. The earthwork and ditch can be traced up the hill to the south on its marathon trek to Chepstow. The deer park of **Chirk Castle** is on the north side of the valley. Built by Roger Mortimer four centuries after the neighbouring Dyke, this is the only border castle to have been continually inhabited since it was built in the late thirteenth century. Border it certainly is, being almost within hailing distance of England. It has been lived in by the Myddleton family since 1595 but is in the care of the National Trust and open to the public in season. The interior of the castle boasts splendid staterooms, but the extensive grounds and park are worth a visit in themselves.

The village of Pontfadog straddles the road and it is only a short way from there to **Glyn Ceiriog**, the main settlement in the valley. For many years the slate quarries north of the village provided most of the employment but fulling, the process of turning woven material into flannel, was also important. The village had a thriving cultural life and the Ceiriog Memorial Institute was built in 1911 in honour of the valley's poets, such as Huw 'Eos' Morus. George Borrow came in search of Morus' home on his epic journey round Wales in 1854. In his book 'Wild Wales' he records a walk from Llangollen, five miles over the hills to the north. It was over this ancient route that Borrow sought the company of a local man, John Jones, partly for protection against the 'Gwyddelians' (Irish) who occupied parts of the hillside.

At Glyn Ceiriog the valley turns sharply south, its character changing as it enters a gorge. The steeper sides, strewn with scattered rocks and covered with bracken herald the upper reaches of the valley and the route into the wilder uplands of the Berwyn. The name **Pandy** indicates the village's importance as a fulling mill, which made locally woven wool into flannel. The mill, possibly the oldest of its kind in Wales, is now the Woolpack, on the east side of the road. The outcrop of Pandy Crag dominates the valley here. An eruption of underwater volcanoes 500 million years ago resulted in deposits of tuffs, which can be seen here and in several other locations locally. Many minerals have been quarried in the area including silica and slate.

The track bed of the Glyn Valley Tramway is also evident here. Originally a horse drawn narrow gauge line, it was opened in 1872. It originally ran from the canal quay at Chirk to Glyn Ceiriog but was later extended up the valley. The tramway converted to steam in 1888 and its primary role was to service local industries, such as the giant Hendre granite quarry between Pandy and Tregeiriog. However, passengers were also carried for most of its lifetime. A serious flood washed part of the line away on 21st December 1900 but it remained in use until the mid 1930s. Some of the track bed is now owned by the National Trust and it forms part of the Ceiriog Valley walk from Chirk to Llanarmon DC.

A little further on you can glimpse the enormous dark chasm of Hendre Quarry across the river in the woods on the east bank. Opened in 1875, the quarry provided granite for use in road building. It was open until 1950 and employed over 100 men. The valley is a place rich in natural interest. The bracken clad steep slopes of the upper valley are dotted with foxgloves; while on the floor of the valley patches of woodland provide habitats for hedgerow plants, with birdsong always haunting the air.

The village of **Llanarmon Dyffryn Ceiriog** lies across a bridge on the southern bank of the river. It's the last significant settlement in the valley, though a mountain road leads over to Llanrhaeadr-ym-Mochnant and the Tanat valley. Another ancient route, the Ffordd Saeson, comes across the hills from the Dee valley at Llandrillo. It is said that Henry II traversed the bleak pass of Pen Bwlch Llandrillo in treacherous weather during 1165. It makes an adventurous, but not unduly arduous, ten-mile journey across the ridge of the Berwyn. Llandrillo is served by some buses on route X94 so a linear walk is a possibility, though proper mountain equipment and precautions are needed, as the terrain is desolate and lonely.

The village has always been a strategic, if remote, junction. For centuries, drovers would stay here on their journey to England. The church is an ancient religious site and St Garmon, a wandering French evangelist and bishop, established the church. There are two yew trees in the churchyard over 1000 years old. The poet John 'Ceiriog' Hughes, farm hand turned poet, was born in the valley in 1832.

Much of this upper valley would have been under water had it not been for the intervention of Lloyd George. In 1923 there was a proposal to create two large reservoirs either side of Llanarmon to serve the breweries of Warrington. Eighty-two houses would have been submerged but a vigorous campaign was launched to oppose the project. 'The English are taking the W out of Wales and turning it into ales' ran the lyrics of one campaign song. Lloyd George, though a native of Gwynedd, had a particular affection for the Ceiriog valley and championed the opposition in Parliament. 'There are plenty of desolate moorlands in Wales. Why should they pick out this exquisite little valley of the Ceiriog?' As Prime Minister at the time he carried considerable clout and the scheme fell.

Route Information

Section	Bus No.	Operator	Weekday frequency	Sunday frequency	Jny Time	Rover tickets
Oswestry - Chirk - Glyn Ceiriog - Llanarmon DC	60	GHA	7 journeys to Glyn Ceiriog, 2 journeys extend to Llanarmon	No service	Chirk - Llanarmon 25 min	FPN TT
Wrexham - Chirk - Glyn Ceiriog - Llanarmon DC	65	GHA	4 journeys	No service		FPN TT
Llangollen - Chirk - Glyn Ceiriog	64	Bryn Melyn	8 journeys	No service		FPN TT

Places to Visit

Chirk Castle and Gardens   01691-777701
www.nationaltrust.org.uk

Upper Mills Trout Farm, Glyn Ceiriog   01691-718225
www.trout-farm.co.uk

Ideas for Walking
The Ceiriog Valley Walk follows the valley from Chirk to Llanarmon. You can use the bus to leave or join the path at a number of points.

The circular Ceiriog Trail (23 miles) and the Upper Ceiriog Trail (14 miles) have been designed for horse riders, mountain bikes and walkers.

You could walk between Glyn Ceiriog and Llangollen using the ancient lane and bridleway called Allt y Badi over the hill (4 miles) and return by bus.

There are more adventurous linear possibilities using a bus to return. These require mountain equipment and precautions. Ffordd Saeson leads from Llanarmon over the Berwyn to Llandrillo in the Dee valley. Journey J gives details of the buses here. To use buses you would be best to start and finish in Wrexham or Ruabon, using the X94 for Llandrillo and the 65 for Llanarmon.

Refreshments

Two pubs in Llanarmon DC cater for visitors offering food and accommodation. Other facilities are situated in Glyn Ceiriog and Chirk.

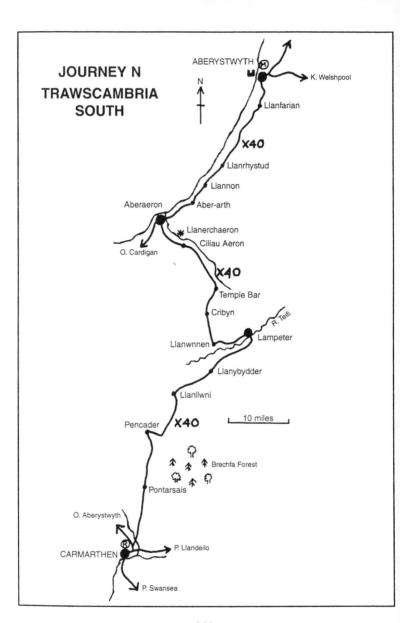

JOURNEY N
TRAWSCAMBRIA
SOUTH

N

ABERYSTWYTH

K. Welshpool

Llanfarian

X40

Llanrhystud

Llannon

Aberaeron   Aber-arth

O. Cardigan   Llanerchaeron

Ciliau Aeron

X40

Temple Bar

Cribyn

R. Teifi

Llanwnnen   Lampeter

Llanybydder

Llanllwni

10 miles

Pencader   X40

Brechfa Forest

Pontarsais

O. Aberystwyth

CARMARTHEN   P. Llandeilo

P. Swansea

Journey N: Trawscambria South

Aberystwyth – Lampeter – Carmarthen

A regular train service used to run between Aberystwyth and Carmarthen. It must have been a scenic gem, steaming through Tregaron, Lampeter and Pencader before connecting at Carmarthen with the South Wales main line to Cardiff and beyond. The service was withdrawn in 1965. If you want to travel by train from Aberystwyth to Carmarthen today you must engage in a 200-mile odyssey through Shrewsbury, Cardiff and Swansea. The disjointed residue of the Welsh railway network underlines the importance of strategic bus services in the country.

The direct route between Aberystwyth and Carmarthen is the successor to this old railway line, providing a key public transport link between mid and South Wales. This is now branded with the name of 'TrawsCambria'.

Aberystwyth to Aberaeron

The sea front at **Aberystwyth** peers westward across the great sweep of Cardigan Bay. On a clear evening you can see from Pembrokeshire to Llŷn, with the distinctive whaleback shape of Bardsey beckoning from the extreme northwest tip of Wales. The town commands a charming situation, at the mouth of two rivers with the hills and forests of an unspoilt hinterland rising behind. The first university college in Wales was established here in 1872 with just 29 students and two staff housed in the rather severe Gothic Old College building on the sea front. The university now educates some 8000 students from across the world and occupies a commanding position on Penglais Hill above the town. On the same hillside is the

National Library of Wales, opened in 1937, home to many old manuscripts including the earliest copy of the Mabinogion. The promenade curves along the sea front, decorated by flags representing minority Celtic languages and the nations of the European Union. A cliff railway climbs from its northern end to Constitution Hill, from where you can view the surrounding countryside through the world's biggest Camera Obscura. A local tradition of kicking the railings at the northern end of the prom apparently originates from a royal visitor who put his foot on the railing while looking at the cliffs. At the opposite end of the promenade a harbour and new marina stand by the mouth of the river Rheidol. Aberystwyth Castle interrupts the graceful curve of the promenade. Built by Edward I in 1277, it was captured by Owain Glyndŵr in 1404, who used it as an administrative and military base until its recapture four years later. Today the attractive rocky knoll also includes a bardic stone circle erected in 1916 to mark the annual meeting of the National Eisteddfod. The nearby pier was built in 1864 but a mighty storm in 1938 reduced its length by 200 feet to its present 700.

You leave Aberystwyth by climbing to the east of Pendinas hill, site of an iron-age fort. This is over 2000 years old, though the monument on top dates only from 1852 and commemorates the Duke of Wellington. At Llanfarian the river Ystwyth is crossed as it nears the end of its journey from the Cambrian Mountains. From here to Llanrhystud, the road follows an inland course with frequent undulations, and fields rather than cliffs provide the scenery.

The river Wyre, crossed at **Llanrhystud**, is sometimes seen by linguists as the border between the Goidel and Brythonic branches of Celtic language and tradition.

Writing in the nineteenth century, the painter Turner observed that, 'different habits and different racial distinctions are still noticeable.' Between Llanrhystud and Aberaeron, the coast offers a string of excellent sandy beaches. Not surprisingly, the sea has determined the fate of many communities on this coast. In the eighteenth and nineteenth centuries, **Llanon** enjoyed prosperity through shipbuilding and farming. Its abundant barley crops were fertilised by seaweed, harvested from the beaches. South of Llanon, the road maintains a high level for most of the way before dropping down to the village of Aberarth. There are wide views across the bay to enjoy from the window. You may be lucky enough to spot porpoises out to sea. Soon after Aberarth, another descent leads into the bustling Georgian harbour town of Aberaeron.

Aberaeron to Carmarthen

Aberaeron was just a small fishing hamlet until 1805 when plans were drawn up to build a new harbour here. The town soon became a wealthy port and shipbuilding centre. Today the colourful houses and broad, planned streets of the town witness to its prosperity and make the town an attractive base.

At Aberaeron, the X40 turns inland, tracing the Aeron valley away from the sea. This is fertile country and the eighteenth century mansion of **Llanerchaeron**, just to the north of the route, indicates the wealth of local gentry at the time. The villa was built in 1795 and was designed by John Nash. Today the estate is a working organic farm in the care of the National Trust and open to visitors. Two restored walled gardens provide herbs and fruit and there are walks through the extensive parkland. Local land yields dairy produce, evident from the cheese producers around Ystrad Aeron. The top of the Aeron valley is reached around Felinfach and then it's a descent into the catchment of the Teifi. A pretty but sinuous route winds through Cribyn and down the valley of the Grannell to reach Llanwnnen. A short ride along the Teifi valley brings you to the university town of Lampeter.

Strictly speaking, **Lampeter** has only been a university town since 1971. But its educational pedigree is much older. The first students were admitted to St David's College on St David's Day in 1827, making it one of the oldest educational institutions in Wales and England. The college maintained close links with the church and remains an important centre for theological education today, though it became part of the University of Wales in 1971. Dylan Thomas, who stayed with friends nearby and lodged in the Castle Hotel, often visited this part of Wales. Although academia and tourism provide much of Lampeter's livelihood, the town is still a centre for the agricultural communities around and retains many features and events of a rural market town.

You cross the Teifi as you leave Lampeter and the bridge also marks the boundary between Ceredigion and Carmarthenshire. The river meanders through fields nearby and remains as our companion as far as **Llanybydder**. This small market town hosts a monthly horse fair. Undulating country follows and the wild uplands of the Brechfa Forest loom up to the east. **Pencader** is another agricultural community, rich in history. The remains of a motte and bailey castle probably date from 1145. Henry II came here to receive the allegiance of the local lord a few years later but was accosted by an elderly man. A plaque in Welsh records the events, as chronicled in 1163 by Gerald of Wales. 'My Lord king, this nation may now be harassed, weakened and decimated by your soldiery, as it has so often been by others in former times; but it will never be totally destroyed by the wrath of man, unless at the same time it is punished by the wrath of God. Whatever else may come to pass, I do not think that on the Day of Direst Judgement any race other than the Welsh, or any other language, will give answer to the Supreme Judge of all for this small corner of the earth.' Certainly the language has well outlived the Plantagenet monarchy. The road crosses a succession of streams and rivers descending from afforested hills, including the Gwili at Pontarsais. A patchwork of fields bounded by flourishing hedgerows covers the countryside and, south of Peniel, the hills give way to the Tywi valley on the approach to Carmarthen. *Carmarthen is described in Journey O. You can return to Aberystwyth via Journey O, making an interesting circular route.*

Route Information

Section	Bus No.	Operator	Weekday frequency	Sunday frequency	Jny Time	Rover tickets
Aberystwyth - Lampeter - Carmarthen	X40	Arriva Cymru/ First Cymru	Hourly (2 journeys extend to Cardiff)	1 journey	2 hours 20 min	FPS* WW

NOTES
Additional services between Aberaeron and Aberystwyth (X50, 550) - see Journey O.
* Flexipass not valid on extension to Cardiff

Places to Visit

National Library of Wales, Aberystwyth   01970-632800
www.llgc.org.uk

Ceredigion Museum, Aberystwyth   01970-633088

Cliff Railway, Aberystwyth   01970-617642
                    www.aberystwythcliffrailway.co.uk

Aberaeron Sea Aquarium   01545-570142

Llanerchaeron Estate   01545-570200
                    www.nationaltrust.org.uk/wales

Carmarthen Museum, Abergwili   01267-223830

Ideas for Walking
Enjoy a cliff walk from Aberaeron. Some stimulating cliff
paths offer good views across Cardigan Bay. Details are
available from the Tourist Information Centre at the
harbour or from other TICs in Ceredigion.

Refreshments
There is a full range of facilities in Aberystwyth and
Carmarthen. Intermediate stops could be made in
Aberaeron or Lampeter which both host a selection of
places to eat.

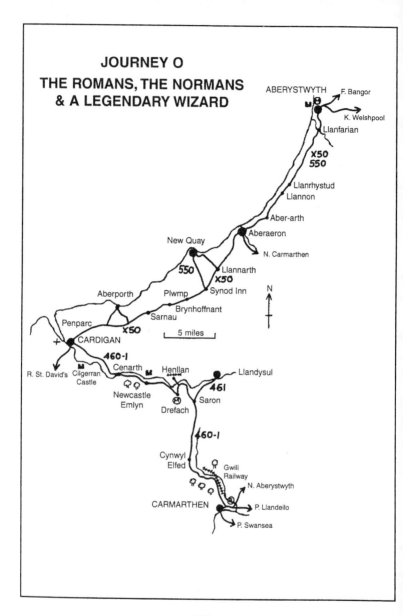

JOURNEY O
THE ROMANS, THE NORMANS
& A LEGENDARY WIZARD

ABERYSTWYTH   F. Bangor

K. Welshpool

Llanfarian

X50
550

Llanrhystud
Llannon

Aber-arth

New Quay   Aberaeron

N. Carmarthen

550

Llannarth
X50

Synod Inn

N

Aberporth   Plwmp

Brynhoffnant

Sarnau

5 miles

Penparc

X50

CARDIGAN

R. St. David's   460-1

Cilgerran
Castle   Cenarth   Henllan   Llandysul

Newcastle
Emlyn   461

Drefach   Saron

460-1

Cynwyl
Elfed   Gwili
Railway

N. Aberystwyth

CARMARTHEN   P. Llandeilo

P. Swansea

Journey O: The Romans, The Normans and a Legendary Wizard

Carmarthen – Cardigan –Aberystwyth

Legends surround Carmarthen, which claims to be the oldest town in Wales. The Roman fort of Moridunum and legendary home of Merlin is the starting point for this trip. The route climbs the wooded Gwili valley and crosses dairy country to reach the Teifi. History abounds here with a woollen museum, coracle centre and two restored railway lines. The coastal town of Cardigan was fortified by the Normans and is still an important centre today. North of here you're never far from the coast and, if you're lucky, could catch a glimpse of bottle nosed dolphins in the bay. You can combine this trip with Journey N to make an interesting circular route, all for the price of a West Wales Rover.

The town of **Carmarthen** is smothered in layers of ancient legend. One story tells how the wizard Merlin ('Myrddin' in Welsh) was born in a cave near the town, giving his name to a nearby hill, Bryn Myrddin, and possibly even to the town itself (Caerfyrddin). Such legends are always disputed and often disparaged. But scratch the surface of modern scepticism and a streak of folk superstition clings on in the deep emotion of modern humanity. The tree known as 'Merlin's Oak' was said to hold the fate of Carmarthen in its roots. If the tree fell, the town itself would fall. Faced with its imminent demise under a new road, the tree was recently dug up and lodged in a local museum, just in case of any veracity in the old tale. The Black Book of Carmarthen is a collection of folk tales and makes reference to some of the old Arthurian legends, but

Carmarthen's history lies deeper still. Carmarthen claims to be the oldest town in Wales. It is certainly marinated in antiquity and was the westernmost Roman settlement in the country. The Roman town of Moridunum, meaning seaport, was a fort built here in 75AD, though by 130 the Roman army had left. The remains of a 5000-seater amphitheatre can be seen to the east of the town centre.

Leaving Carmarthen Bus Station, the bus passes below the remains of the Norman castle, now colonised by the council offices. It heads west past the remains of the Roman amphitheatre to the hospital. Here the route heads north up Gwili valley. The preserved **Gwili Railway** is one of two working remnants of the Carmarthen and Cardigan railway dating from 1860. In fact the line itself only reached Newcastle Emlyn, though it also led to Aberystwyth via Pencader Junction. Today the restored section of line accompanies the bus route and road along the bottom of the Gwili valley for just over two miles from Bronwydd Arms station. The road winds through the thickly wooded gorge with the steep rocky slopes of Allt Crych-du rising up to farmland above. The river is an ideal spot for dippers and kingfishers while rich hedgerows provide habitats for a variety of wild flowers. After Cwmduad the road climbs out of the valley and crosses more open country before dropping down through Rhos and Saron into the Teifi valley.

Some buses leave the main road at Saron to serve the town of Llandysul. The market town nestles on the banks of the Teifi, centred round its church. St Tysul was a cousin of St David and lived from 462 to 544. He was also grandson of Ceredog who gave his name to Ceredigion. Some connections! Before the days of electricity, the waters of the river provided the energy to drive many waterwheels in the area. During the Civil War, royalists defending Ceredigion from the parliamentary forces pulled down one of the bridge's three arches to prevent their opponents from crossing the river.

After Saron, the bus reaches Henllan where another stub of the old railway has been restored and reopened as the **Teifi Valley Railway**. Steam trains run two miles through woods to Llandyfriog. The line was originally a branch from Pencader to Newcastle Emlyn. Just across the river, Dre-fach is home to the **National Woollen Museum**. The community was once the focus of a thriving textile industry and produced clothing, hosiery and blankets. The museum tells the story, illustrated with collections and displays. Traditional Welsh fabrics are also produced in the museum.

Returning to the main road and the Teifi at Pentrecagal, it's now just a short ride into the busy market town of **Newcastle Emlyn**. The town is charmingly situated in a loop in the river Teifi. Inside the loop the stone stumps of the old castle dating from around 1240 lie on a grassy mound. The 'new' castle distinguishes the fortress from the 'old' castle at Cilgerran, near Cardigan.

The Teifi remains our companion almost all the way to Cardigan as the road follows the valley towards the sea. At **Cenarth**, a series of waterfalls makes a picturesque scene just upstream from the seventeenth-century bridge. Nearby a museum traces the history of the coracle. The simple boat has been used in Wales since the Bronze Age but, although something of a Celtic icon, the craft actually originates in Asia. One was used in the escape of the Dalai Lama from Tibet. The bus follows the flood plain of the Teifi as far as **Llechryd**. A nature reserve accompanies the river downstream from Llechryd's bridge as far as Cilgerran, aiming to conserve the ancient oak woodland that clings to the spectacular gorge. However, the main road and bus route head directly for Cardigan and the salty taste of the estuary.

Cardigan to Aberystwyth

You will need to change buses at Cardigan to continue north along the coast. From here you can also travel south-west into the Pembrokeshire national park *(see Journey R)*.

Cardigan lies a couple of miles upstream from the mouth of the Teifi and the bridge here provides the lowest crossing point of the river. The town was founded in 1093 when the Normans built a castle. The remains crown a rocky mount above the bridge but the grounds are private. In the nineteenth century Cardigan became an important port, trading with Ireland and shipping emigrants to Canada. Two hundred ships were built here during the century, though the coming of railways and the silting of the estuary led to its decline. The port only finally closed in 1981. The attractive High Street straddles a ridge and a maze of smaller streets and alleys branch down from the main thoroughfare. A short way downstream, St Dogmael's Abbey dates from the twelfth century. The ruins are cared for by Cadw and can be visited.

North of Cardigan, the bus route follows the main road for some way. Although this road shadows the coast, it generally keeps a few miles inland until Aberaeron. The undulating, dairy country is pleasant. Felinwynt Rainforest Centre lies a mile or so off the route with tropical butterflies flying free in the tropical house. Buses divert to the coast at Aberporth, leaving the main road to serve this attractive seaside village. The community is also home to an RAF base, the Defence, Test and

Evaluation Organisation. Bottlenose dolphins are regularly seen in Cardigan Bay. It is estimated that about 130 are resident in the bay and south Ceredigion is one of the best places to view them. Regaining the main road at Tan-y-groes, progress north continues through a series of small villages such as Brynhoffnant and Plwmp to reach the Synod Inn.

Synod Inn is one of those places where a pub has given its name to a community. It is an unremarkable place but a celebrated location on the Welsh bus network. Its unceremonious bus shelter has long been a key connecting point for buses between Cardigan, Aberystwyth, New Quay and Lampeter. From here the TrawsCambria service X50 continues north on the main road towards Aberystwyth. Other services on route 550 return to the coast to serve the popular holiday resort of **New Quay**. The 'new quay' dates from the late seventeenth century and was replaced by the small pier on the far side of the sandy beach. The town has a history of coastal trading, fishing and boat building. Latterly, it is as a holiday resort that it is best known. The small streets lead down to the pier and sea front, popular with families and surfers.

Buses serving New Quay rejoin the main road at Llanarth and continue along the switchback A487, tantalisingly close to the sea, but far enough away to deprive you of any views. A long descent leads to Aberaeron, where the TrawsCambria route from Carmarthen is joined.

The route from here to Aberystwyth follows the sea more closely and you can find details of this section at the beginning of Journey P.

Route Information

!! Warning

Some reworking of the complicated timetable on the
X50/550 seems possible

Section	Bus No.	Operator	Weekday frequency	Sunday frequency	Jny Time	Rover tickets
Carmarthen - Cardigan	460 461	First Cymru/ Richards Bros	7 journeys (some additional short workings)	No service	1 hour 30 min	FPS WW
Cardigan - Aberystwyth	X50	Richards Bros	8 journeys but some terminate at Aberaeron	No service	1 hour 40 min	FPS WW
Cardigan - New Quay - Aberystwyth	550	Arriva Cymru/ Richards Bros	Every 2 hours (Hourly New Quay - Aberystwyth)	4 journeys summer 2 journeys winter	2 hours	RR FPS

Places to visit

Gwili Railway, Bronwydd Arms Station   01267-230666
                                    www.gwili-railway.co.uk

National Woollen Museum, Dre-fach Felindre
                                            01559-370929
                                            www.nmgw.ac.uk

Teifi Valley Railway, Henllan   01559-371077
                                    www.teifivalleyrailway.co.uk

The National Coracle Centre, Cenarth Falls
                                            01239-710980
                                    www.coracle-centre.co.uk

St Dogmael's Abbey, Cardigan   01443-336000
www.cadw.wales.gov.uk
Felinwynt Rainforest Centre, Cardigan   01239 810250
www.butterflycentre.co.uk

Ideas for Walking
Ceredigion has a similar potential to Pembrokeshire for coastal walks. There is no continuous footpath but there are excellent stretches of cliff path. One section follows the cliffs south out of Aberaeron. A guide is available from the Tourist Information Centre in the harbour.

Refreshments
The major places on this route all make good stopovers for refreshments or exploration. Aberaeron, Cardigan and Newcastle Emlyn all have plenty to tempt the visitor.

JOURNEY P
CARMARTHENSHIRE

Journey P: Carmarthenshire

Carmarthen – Llandeilo – Swansea – Llanelli – Carmarthen

Carmarthenshire is a stronghold of the Welsh language. In fact more people speak Welsh here than any other county in Wales. Unlike the north, where the country comprises rural communities and small towns, Carmarthenshire abuts some of the most densely populated and industrialised areas of the country. This tour offers a cross section of rural and urban Wales. It takes in the fertile farming land of the Tywi valley, the former mining communities of the Dulais valley, the wide coastal panoramas of the Loughor and Pembrey Forest and Wales' bustling second city.

Carmarthen to Llandeilo

Carmarthen is a busy town and offers much of interest. Leaving the bus station, you pass beneath the walls of the old Norman castle, with the council offices occupying a mock French chateau built inside its fortifications. Leaving through the suburbs, you pass near the Roman amphitheatre that once entertained an audience of 5000. Before leaving the town the route diverts to serve the West Wales Hospital. *You can read about Carmarthen in Journey O.*

Abergwili became the home of bishops of St David's from 1542. The location was perhaps more convenient than the eponymous base of their see, flung out on its isolated peninsula forty miles to the west. The palace occupies wooded ground above the river Tywi and was rebuilt at the beginning of the twentieth century. It is now home to the Carmarthenshire Museum, which interprets the agricultural and social history of the county. The Romans mined gold around here and some of the jewellery on display is made from this ancient treasure. The palace chapel is also open to the public.

Just beyond Abergwili, a steep wooded hill swoops down to the north side of the road. This is **Bryn Myrddin**, or Merlin's Hill, acclaiming Carmarthen's mythical connections with the mysterious figure of Merlin and the name given to a rousing traditional Welsh hymn. It looks out across the pastoral lands of the Tywi valley with the river meandering through meadows and fields in no great haste to reach anywhere. In contrast, the main road presses relentlessly east, crossing tributaries draining the hills of Brechfa Forest to the north. On the far side of the valley, Paxton's Tower dominates a wooded ridge, while the remains of Dryslwyn Castle crown a mound commanding a crossing point of the river. **Aberglasney**'s restored gardens date from the late sixteenth century and lie just to the south of Broad Oak. Rare features include a gatehouse and yew tunnel. Ornamental and walled gardens can also be explored.

Llandeilo to Swansea

It is possible to continue to Llandovery on this bus. Connections can be made from there to Brecon. But to continue with this tour, you need to change buses at Llandeilo.

Llandeilo sits on the edge of Dinefwr Park. The name of Dinefwr echoes down the ages of Welsh history as the seat of the kings of Deheubarth, among them Rhodri Mawr and the great lawmaker Hywel Dda. The remains of the imposing medieval castle, clinging to a rocky crag, became an English royal prize after the conquest of Edward I. A house was rebuilt here in 1660 and has been recently restored. It's the parkland that is Dinefwr's glory, with acres of deer park and walks so attractive that Capability Brown refused to make any substantial alterations, declaring that, 'nature has been truly bountiful.'

Llandeilo Parish Church is a reminder of the Christian history of this small town. St Teilo founded a monastery here in the 6th century. A legend tells of how the saint rescued seven children from drowning and brought them here where they in turn grew into saints. The tower of the church is over 700 years old. Nearby, Georgian and Victorian buildings are evidence of the prosperity of the area over centuries.

Passing the church, the road drops down past a row of colourful cottages to cross the Tywi. Upstream from here is the railway bridge carrying the Heart of Wales railway line between Swansea and Llanelli. Passing through Ffairfach, a climb through the wooded Cennen valley brings us past Cilyrchen quarry to Llandybie. **Ammanford** is just a short distance from here. The town was built on coal, and the need for transport also led to the construction of an extensive local rail network. Until 1880, the community was known as Cross Inn. The name was changed to avoid confusion with other similarly named communities. But it also finally ended the embarrassment felt by local teetotal chapels, forced to include the name of a public house on the church notice board. The geographically descriptive 'Ammanford' was the name chosen in preference to the obsequiously deferential 'Dinefwr', which recalled the local earl and landlord. The town is one of the strongest Welsh-speaking towns in the south, with over 75% of the population fluent in the language.

Between Ammanford and Pontarddulais the route climbs out of the Amman Valley through a series of satellite communities. It leaves the main road to contour round the hillside overlooking the Gwili valley and Pont Abraham, birthplace of the M4 at the beginning of its eastward odyssey to London. Passing through the village of Llanedi the route drops down the ridge to cross the river Dulais. The bridge crosses not only into **Pontarddulais** but also into the City and County of Swansea.

Urban scenery becomes more apparent south of Pontarddulais. Climbing through Pontlliw the road crosses the M4 at Penllergaer. A dual carriageway and increased traffic indicates the advance of the city, confirmed by the inevitable retail park at Fforest Fach. Rows of terraced houses and estates curve round the hillsides as the altitude drops and Swansea's railway terminus at High Street marks the start of the city centre.

Swansea to Carmarthen

Minerals lie at the heart of **Swansea**'s history. For hundreds of years shallow coal seams had been exploited but it was during the eighteenth century that the mouth of the Tawe became a focus for industry. A burgeoning metropolis grew around mining coal and smelting lead, zinc and copper. Access to the sea gave the town its role as a port until the docks were closed in 1969. A major regeneration scheme turned these decaying relics into a new marina and leisure area named the Maritime Quarter. A new Waterfront Museum opened in 2005, while the Maritime and Industrial Museum based here interprets the geographical and historical context of Swansea and its hinterland. The castle is a reminder of the more distant past when Swansea was an Anglo-Norman settlement surrounded by resentful Welsh natives. The Dylan Thomas Centre, housed in the magnificent

Guildhall, reflects the cultural dimension of the city's past and its links with one of Wales' most famous writers. A memorial in Cwmdonkin Park commemorates Thomas' nearby birthplace. Swansea Bay curves westwards from the city centre and a five and a half mile promenade leads to Mumbles Head and the Gower.

The bus to Carmarthen passes the station to begin a steady climb through Cwmbwrla to attain the higher ground to the north of the city. As the suburbs relent, the bus turns west towards the **Loughor estuary**. From this elevation there is a clear prospect across the marshes but soon there's a descent to sea level to cross the Loughor Bridge. The railway is a close companion, the main line being forced to cross this gateway to western Wales on a single-track viaduct. Now the Gower peninsula is clearly seen across the rich wetlands of the Loughor. The National Wetlands Centre Wales, conserves the precious habitats along the estuary. The Millennium Coastal Park has opened up this stretch of coast around Llanelli and a cycle route perambulates through the marshes and dunes all the way to Pembrey. In contrast, the enormous Trostre tinplate works underlines the importance of tin in the history of **Llanelli**, gaining it the title of 'Tinopolis'. Coal and steel were also important elements in Llanelli's history, though in recent decades the town has had to seek new routes to prosperity. Rugby is a proud tradition here but the origin of the term 'Turks' as a nickname for local people is uncertain.

The Millennium Coastal Park continues along the estuary past Llanelli. The bus serves the communities of Burry Port and Pembrey, tumbling through an unremitting ribbon of urban development. The quay at **Burry Port** was built when nearby Pembrey became silted up. Amelia Earhart, the first woman to fly across the

Atlantic, landed near here. **Pembrey Country Park** was opened on the site of a vast military complex but the dunes and forest are now a popular leisure attraction. Over 200 hectares of parkland and eight miles of award-winning clean beaches await exploration.

Leaving the main road at Commissioners' Bridge, buses travel through the historic town of **Kidwelly**, centred around the impressive remains of a Norman castle. The twin-towered gatehouse, dating from 1422, tops a steep bluff above the river Gwendraeth. Originally the fortress was a wooden affair built in 1106 to secure Norman hegemony over the routes west. Like most castles, it was rebuilt in stone in successive centuries. The well-preserved remains give an excellent insight into medieval life.

From Kidwelly, the route turns inland, following the valley of the river Gwendraeth Fach. Climbing out of the valley at Llandyfaelog, higher ground offers views across the Tywi valley and a gentle descent brings us to its lowest crossing point at the historic borough of Carmarthen.

Route Information

Section	Bus No.	Operator	Weekday frequency	Sunday frequency	Jny Time (min)	Rover tickets
Carmarthen - Llandeilo - Llandovery	280 281	First Cymru	7 journeys	No service	45	FPS WW
Llandeilo - Swansea	X13	First Cymru	Every hour (30 min Ammanford - Swansea)	5 journeys	90	FPS WW
Swansea - Carmarthen	X11	First Cymru	Every 30 min	No service	90	FPS WW

Places of Interest

Carmarthen Museum, Abergwili   01267-223830

Aberglasney Gardens   01558-668998
                                  www.aberglasney.org

Dinefwr Park, Llandeilo   01558-823947
                                  www.nationaltrust.org.uk

National Waterfront Museum, Swansea   01792-459640
                                  www.waterfrontmuseum.co.uk

Dylan Thomas Centre, Swansea   01792-463980
                                  www.dylanthomas.org

Swansea Museum   01792-653763
                                  www.swansea.gov.uk

Singleton Park & Botanical Gardens, Swansea
                                  01792-280210

Plantasia, Swansea   01792-474555
                                  www.plantasia.org

Maritime and Industrial Museum, Swansea
                                  01792-650351

National Wetlands Centre Wales, Llanelli
                                  01554-741087
                                  www.wwt.org.uk

Pembrey Country Park   01554-833913

Kidwelly Castle   01554-890104
                                          www.cadw.wales.gov.uk

Ideas for walking

Explore Pembrey Country Park or walk the Millennium Coastal Park near Llanelli. These offer miles of footpaths and cycle ways alongside the Loughor estuary and the sea.

Refreshments

Swansea offers a wide range of places to eat, as you would expect from a major city. You could take a trip to Mumbles on city service 2 to sample some of the restaurants and bars overlooking the rugged Gower peninsula and the wide Bristol Channel. Other intermediate stops such as Ammanford, Llandeilo, Llanelli and Kidwelly also provide places for refreshment.

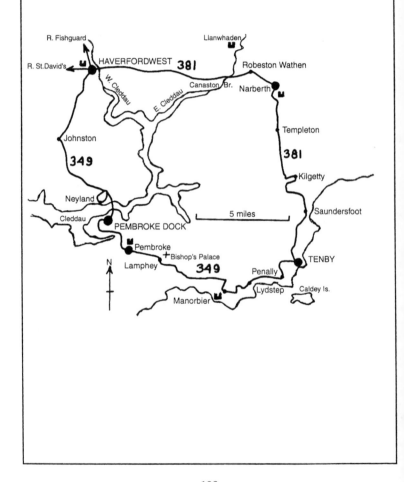

JOURNEY Q
S. PEMBROKESHIRE

R. Fishguard

R. St.David's

HAVERFORDWEST **381**

W. Cleddau

E. Cleddau

Canaston Br.

Llanwhaden

Robeston Wathen

Narberth

Templeton

381

Johnston

349

Neyland

Cleddau

PEMBROKE DOCK

Pembroke

+ Bishop's Palace

Lamphey

349

N

Manorbier

Penally

Lydstep

Caldey Is.

Kilgetty

Saundersfoot

5 miles

TENBY

Journey Q: South Pembrokeshire

Haverfordwest – Narberth – Tenby – Pembroke – Haverfordwest

The Pembrokeshire coastline forms the western seaboard of Wales for nearly 200 miles. And it's the sea that has carved its initials on nearly every aspect of life in a county whose land border is only about a quarter the length of its coast. Across the sea came traders to ports such as Tenby and Haverfordwest. Out of the sea came the fish that sustained the livelihoods of fishermen along the coast. The depth of the sea provides an anchorage for the great oil tankers in Milford Haven, while its shallow reaches offer some of the finest beaches in Wales. Trade, heavy industry, fishing and tourism owe their existence to the sea whose waves incessantly pound the dramatic cliffs and photogenic beaches of the west.

This route offers a taste of all these aspects of south Pembrokeshire's scenery and history. Through Narberth, the stage for some of Wales' oldest legends, to the picturesque walled town of Tenby. Returning along the south coast, the bus passes the ancient castles of Manorbier and Pembroke and offers panoramic views of the Cleddau estuary, Pembrokeshire's own fjord. En route we meet the twelfth century churchman whose guidebook to Wales is still in print today and the Welshman who seized the crown of England and whose descendants included Henry VIII and Queen Elizabeth.

Haverfordwest to Tenby via Narberth

From **Haverfordwest** bus station on the banks of the Western Cleddau, past the railway station, the bustle of Pembrokeshire's county town is soon left behind. Striking out east, this highway is the historic turnpike route from

Fishguard to London, well over 200 miles away. It is a broad, direct route through low, rolling hills and fertile agricultural land. Progress is quick, passing the village of Slebech and then dropping to Canaston Bridge where the Eastern Cleddau is crossed just upstream from the highest tidal reach.

A map reveals the military significance of this territory in times past. The land is dotted with old castles, earthworks and forts. Picton Castle, now a country house, originated as a thirteenth century defence just above the confluence of the two Cleddau estuaries. Three miles upstream from Canaston Bridge, the ruins of Llanwhaden Castle recall the great wealth of the medieval bishops of St David's, whose estates it was built to defend.

The main road is abandoned at Robeston Wathen for the short journey to **Narberth**, a lively, colourful town and the historic centre of this part of Pembrokeshire. It lies on the 'landsker', an informal line marking the Anglicised southern part of the county from the Welsh speaking north. Narberth's antiquity is evident. Some of the ancient folk tales of the Mabinogion were set here in the town that was once home to the Princes of Dyfed. This collection of medieval tales recounts the heroism and tragedy from Welsh and Brythonic legends. The spirit of the Mabinogion still resonates in Welsh music and poetry. An exhibition in the Wilson Museum in Narberth illustrates the significance of this ancient literature.

Descending from the town the remaining ruins of the castle guard the road as it heads south, soon crossing Narberth Bridge. It's something of a switchback ride as the route crosses the grain of the country through an agrarian landscape. But a farm theme park suggests that tourism rather than farming may be the dominant economic preoccupation. The bus loops around **Kilgetty** and a plethora of campsites confirms the approach of the holiday coast. A series of villages host large numbers of visitors to this dramatic and picturesque coastline. **Saundersfoot** grew around a harbour and wide sandy bay at the foot of an attractive wooded valley. Fishing and tourism still draw the crowds and the village is just a short distance from Amroth, situated on the county boundary and at the terminus of the 177-mile coastal path. The path towards Tenby takes a dramatic and interesting course along the cliff tops past Monkstone Point. The road prefers the more sedentary inland route, passing Two Hedges, to arrive in the historic walled town.

Tenby is a crowded place and it is certainly best to arrive by public transport or on foot. In fact the town centre is closed to motor traffic during summer daytimes, though a park and ride service provides access for drivers. If you like drifting around gift shops, there is plenty of tack for all, but somehow it's forgivable and the superficial froth cannot denude the town's marvellous setting. The esplanade crowns steep cliffs commanding views across to Caldey Island. The old town lies within the historic walls and the narrow streets buzz with pavement cafes, though it's not difficult to find a quiet backwater even on a busy summer day. A maze of alleys leads to the photogenic harbour where boats compete to take you on a variety of fishing trips or the 2-mile journey to Caldey Island. The seafront is outstanding, a series of sandy beaches divided by rocky headlands, one of which is capped by the castle ruins. Just below, St Catherine's is a rocky tidal islet hosting the remains of an old fort built to defend Milford Haven. Originally Tenby was a Welsh fort commanding the limestone promontory on which it stands. The Normans fortified it and built the walls around the old town. And it's the French that the citizens of Tenby should perhaps thank for their prosperity and purpose today. After many years as a trading port, the town's renaissance as a tourist resort was born during the eighteenth century, when the Napoleonic wars made travel in Europe impossible. Baths, gardens and boarding houses catered for visitors and have left the legacy of attractive, colourful Georgian houses seen today.

Tenby to Haverfordwest via Pembroke

If you're short of time, this is not the way to travel back to Haverfordwest. It's the long way round, but it's also rich in interest and variety. An hourly bus service enables you to jump on and off and visit a range of places well worth exploration.

Winding down from Tenby's rocky promontory the main road crosses the marshes to reach Penally. From here a ridge of grassy land separates us from the coast, although a myriad of campsites testifies to its immediate proximity. At Lydstep there are stunning views back along the coast and over to Caldey Island.

A pretty but tortuous lane must be negotiated to reach Manorbier. This is a modest challenge for a car but a contorted route for a full size bus. Manorbier is truly charming, lying sheltered just above a sandy inlet, dominated by the substantial remains of a Norman castle. Through the branches of the trees that envelop the ruins, the whitewashed tower of a Norman church perches on the opposite side of a small valley leading to the beach. The castle was the birthplace of Girald de Barri, better known as Giraldus Cambriensis or Gerald of Wales in about 1146. Gerald's own pedigree reflects the complexity and richness of Welsh history. In his blood mingled the genes of Welsh and Norman aristocracy. His career as a scholar and churchman took him on a tour of Wales in an attempt to recruit soldiers for the crusades. The account of this tour gives insights into the social fabric of the country in the twelfth century and is still a popular work. Gerald's ambition to become Bishop of St David's was never realised, perhaps because of his Welsh maternal ancestry. Describing his birthplace, Gerald's account could hardly be bettered today. 'There stands a castle with excellent towers and defences set atop a coastal hill... Between the castle and the church a never failing stream winds its way along a valley, which is strewn with sands by the strong, sea winds. It runs down from a large lake and there is a water mill on its banks. Heaven's breath smells so wooingly well there.' *Cricieth Castle, at the other end of the country, has an exhibition about Gerald (Journey C).*

Another ten minutes or so through the villages of Jameston and Hodgeston and the bus reaches Lamphey. A half-mile walk from the bus stop along a quiet rural avenue brings you to Lamphey Bishop's Palace. Built by bishops of St David's in the thirteenth and fourteenth centuries, Lamphey was a country retreat from the affairs of church and state. Henry de Gower who held the office in the fourteenth century built much of what now remains. Here he, and his successors, could enjoy the lifestyle of a medieval aristocrat, complete with fishponds, orchards and tranquil wooded parkland. The precinct itself encloses over 7 acres of lawn. As well as constructing de Gower's Hall, the best-preserved part of the remains here, he was also responsible for St David's Bishop's Palace, next to the cathedral. Both remains are now in the care of Cadw.

Just past Lamphey the town of Pembroke sits astride a rocky spur overlooking a silted inlet off the Cleddau estuary. Pembroke's single street, now one-way, leads down the ridge from the castle. Westbound traffic circumnavigates the town passing the main car parks, before winding up to the castle. This is traditionally the birthplace of Henry Tudor and the room of his birth is marked by a tableau also showing his mother Margaret of Beaufort who engineered his elevation to the throne. Henry landed not far from here, at Angle, with his army largely made up of French recruits, to wrest the kingdom from the supposed usurper, Richard III. When Richard III fell on the field of battle at Bosworth in Leicestershire in 1485, the Tudor dynasty was founded with the accession of Henry VII. His subsequent marriage to Elizabeth of York sealed the union of the houses of Lancaster and York and the end of the century-long Wars of the Roses. So, with the accession of Henry Tudor, the English throne combined not only Yorkist and Lancastrian, but also Welsh blood. The great round keep of Pembroke Castle dominates the town and, as the pre-eminent stronghold of south-west Wales, has witnessed many other historic moments.

A tortuous route around Pembroke Dock inflicts a compulsory tour of all the suburbs but in a matter of minutes you've arrived at the soul of the town, the waterfront. Like many ports, Pembroke Dock has suffered decline as well as prosperity during its history. Regeneration is the watchword today with a new marina proposed. A regular car ferry to Ireland ensures it's not quite the end of the line as the humble terminus of the single-track branch railway might suggest. Retail park therapy is the most apparent form of regeneration and you pass at least four superstores before leaving the town to climb up to the Cleddau Bridge.

The high level toll bridge offers wonderful views

downstream over the Cleddau estuary, festooned with boats. Distant views of the chimneys of oil refineries and power stations remind you of the importance of this estuary as a deep-water harbour. Upstream the perspective is more pastoral, underlining the ecological significance of the Cleddau. The estuary is a 'ria' or flooded river valley, similar to examples such as the Tamar in south-west England.

The bus route detours to serve the town of Neyland, before returning to the main road at the same point from where it left. You are compensated for this deviation with a spectacular view of the bridge you have just crossed, this time from the edge of the water below its slender span. Climbing back out of Neyland, you rejoin the main road and the bus now sets a direct course through Johnston to Haverfordwest, and the start of your tour.

Route Information

Section	Bus No.	Operator	Weekday frequency	Sunday frequency	Jny Time (min)	Rover tickets
Haverfordwest - Narberth - Tenby	381	Silcox	Hourly	1 journey	60	FPS WW
Tenby - Pembroke - Haverfordwest	349	First Cymru	Hourly	4 journeys (summer) 2 journeys (Winter)	95	FPS WW

Places to Visit

Narberth Museum   01834-861719

Caldey Island   01834-844453
www.caldey-island.co.uk

Manorbier Castle   01834-871394
                          www.manorbiercastle.co.uk

Lamphey Bishop's Palace   01646-672224
                          www.cadw.wales.gov.uk

Pembroke Castle   01646-684585
                          www.pembrokecastle.co.uk

Ideas for walking
If you are near the coast of Pembrokeshire, the coastal footpath can always tempt. The long distance route weaves its way from Amroth to Cardigan providing an ever-changing vista of sea, cliffs and estuaries. For now, why not just try the section between Saundersfoot and Tenby and use the bus to return?

Refreshments
A plethora of establishments in Tenby cater for the needs of many visitors and tourists. But there are plenty of other places to stop too. Try Pembroke, Narberth or Haverfordwest.

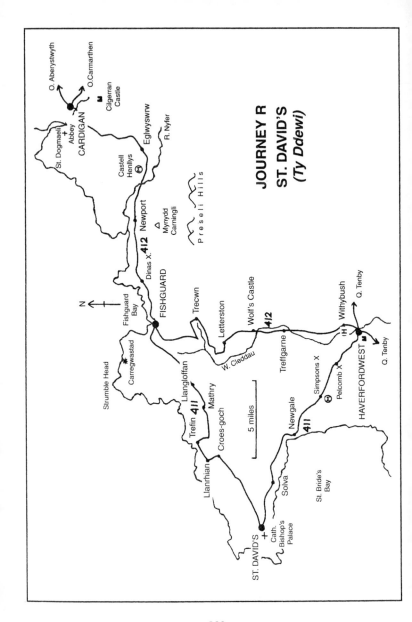

JOURNEY R
ST. DAVID'S
(Ty Ddewi)

Journey R: St David's and the Pembrokeshire Coast

Cardigan – Fishguard – St David's – Haverfordwest – Cardigan

Both saints and invaders have been this way. This is the route to Wales' most holy place, St David's, where the country's patron saint founded a community of monks 1400 years ago. In the Middle Ages, two pilgrimages to St David's gained equal merit to a journey to Rome. Still today, many visitors come as pilgrims and not just as tourists. The long, indented coastline has been the scene of many comings and goings, some in enmity, others in friendship. Perhaps none so bizarre as the chaotic attempt at an invasion by Napoleonic forces in 1797. It is the sea that has moulded the history, heritage and hagiography of this last outpost of Wales, looking out across the western sea.

Cardigan to Fishguard

Crossing the Teifi on the town's elegant 18th century bridge gives you a sense of **Cardigan**'s history and significance. In the nineteenth century the town was an important port, trading with Ireland and shipping emigrants to Canada. Two hundred ships were built here during the century, though the coming of railways and the silting of the estuary led to its decline. The port only finally closed in 1981. The attractive town centre focuses on a ridge topped by the High Street leading to a maze of smaller streets and alleys.

The bus route follows the main road, which climbs out of the Teifi valley, attaining high ground with panoramic views across the surrounding countryside. Down in the valley, a couple of miles east, **Cilgerran Castle** crowns a rocky crag overlooking a wooded gorge. Two circular towers protect its landward sides, while the remainder relied on the steep ravine of the Teifi. Although the castle is not visible from this bus route, another regular service makes the short journey from Cardigan.

The **Preseli Mountains** lie to the south. Purple heather covers the hills and their shimmering bulk broods over the surrounding countryside. It was from these hills that the stones used to build Stonehenge were hewn. The eight- tonne bluestones were transported across rivers and land to Salisbury Plain 200 miles away. The highest ground on the Preseli Mountains is dotted with numerous prehistoric stone circles, sacred sites for the Neolithic tribes who lived here.

One prehistoric site lies nearer the road. As the route descends towards the Nyfer valley, you catch a glimpse of some reconstructed huts across the valley to the north. This is **Castell Henllys**, a 2,300 year-old iron-age fort, once home to about 100 families. Archaeologists have excavated this site over two decades and have rebuilt thatched Iron Age round houses, a smithy and a grain store from their original foundations. The National Park Authority manages the site and it's open to visitors.

Dropping to the river Nyfer at Felindre, a twisty wooded section of road leads soon to **Newport**, a town built by the Normans, their castle now a private residence. Above the town rises Carn Ingli, its serrated ridge capped with the striking remains of forts and hut circles. It is here that the Irish divine, St Brynach, is said to have spoken with angels.

The section of route between Newport and Fishguard offers the best coastal panoramas in south-west Wales. Generally the road maintains a high level and commands some stunning views along the coast. As you approach Fishguard, you may see a ship or high-speed 'sea-cat' arriving from Rosslare in Ireland, just 60 miles away.

A steep winding descent demands good brakes and driving skills as a windy road leads to Fishguard's Lower Town where you cross the river Gwaun, from which the town gains it's Welsh name, Abergwaun. The main part of the town lies up the other side of the slope. To get to St David's you normally need to change buses here.

Fishguard to St David's
Fishguard once hoped to take Liverpool's transatlantic trade and Holyhead's Irish commerce. At the beginning of the twentieth century, the Great Western Railway blasted 2 million tons of rock from the cliffs at Goodwick to create a 600-metre breakwater and a new harbour. Trains still arrive periodically at the harbour station, but the grand dream never really became a reality. However, Fishguard still remains one of the key British ports for travellers to Ireland with regular crossings every day. Day trips are possible too.

The cliffs beyond Goodwick will also be long remembered as the venue for a strange military skirmish. In 1797, four French ships arrived off Fishguard in an attempt to invade Britain. Shots from the local fort deterred a landing in the bay but the shambolic force of 600 men landed at **Carregwastad** a few miles to the west. The poorly disciplined troops seemed to have spent more time drinking wine and stealing chickens than subverting the Hanoverian dynasty. Gleeful embellishments of history assert that the French were sent packing at the sight of women in traditional Welsh costume, mistaking their red cloaks for the red coats of the grenadiers. One such woman, Jemima Nicholas, captured 12 Frenchmen with a pitchfork. However apocryphal the stories, the invaders promptly signed the surrender papers and the curious incident has gone down in history as the 'last invasion of Britain'.

The country beyond Fishguard is different and there is a sense of approaching the Welsh 'Land's End' as you traverse agricultural country of the most westerly peninsula in the country. Wilder country is never far. Just north of the road lies Strumble Head, capped by its lighthouse, marking the southern end of Cardigan Bay.

The village of **Mathry** lies just off the main road on the top of a small hill. The village claims to have seven saints. An old story tells of a man called Cynnanwy whose wife had seven children in one year. Such overwhelming fertility unsurprisingly led to poverty. Being unable to feed the brood, they decided to drown them but were stopped by St Teilo. He took them to Llandeilo to care for them, food being supplied by eight fish, which appeared in the river daily, and one for the saint. As healthy adults, all seven returned to Mathry to preach about God's love. They are reputedly buried in the churchyard. More recently, the village was birthplace for John Brown Evans, the inventor of barbed wire.

St David's to Haverfordwest

Although the road is a few miles inland, the influence of the coast is never far. There are few trees here, and signs point to the villages on the coast such as Trefin and Porthgain. **St David's** appears out of nowhere. It's meant to be that way. Its founders placed the city, with its dramatic cathedral, in a dip to avoid detection. It's a bustling place, full of holidaymakers but also with a vibrant life of its own.

Jutting out into the Atlantic, St David's peninsula has

been home to prehistoric hunters and farmers since the dawn of humanity. The standing stones, mysterious dolmens and remains of ancient settlements lie scattered along the rocky gorse-clad heath. Centuries later, the peninsula became the 'holy land' of Wales, drawing medieval and modern pilgrims to this rocky and windswept extremity of Britain. An ancient story tells how David, the missionary and patron saint of Wales, was born overlooking the sea at a place now known as St Non's Bay. Non gave birth to David on this exposed cliff top during a thunderstorm. A spring of water gushed forth as Nature's response to the event, a frequent device of Celtic hagiography. Blessed with healing properties, it became known as St Non's Well. Whatever the truth of the mythology, the well is surrounded by flowers and lovingly tended and can be visited by a short walk from St David's.

St David established his community of Celtic monks here fourteen hundred years ago. In the middle ages, two journeys to St David's were considered of equal merit to one pilgrimage to Rome. St David's itself, the smallest city in Britain, boasts a remarkable medieval cathedral and lively community. You can visit both the cathedral, and the adjacent Bishop's Palace, now in the care of Cadw. Unlikely as it seems today, this was a major crossroads in Celtic Britain. Boats from Ireland, Cornwall, Brittany, and further field had to pass close to the rocky shores of western Wales. Saints, pilgrims, traders and warriors, all have passed this way. And today, it is a place of strategic importance for many species of sea bird, with a number of internationally important reserves on off shore islands. Boat trips are available to the RSPB reserve on Ramsey Island and around the coast. In spring, the cliffs come alive with a display of flowers that prove the superiority of nature over any handcrafted suburban garden.

The bus leaves the city, passing the excellent National Park Information Centre, which is also where the local Celtic Coaster buses depart from. It's a short journey to Solva, a picturesque village at the end of a natural inlet in the cliffs. It's a steep climb in or out of **Solva** and the deep valley was carved by melting water from glaciers. It has formed a sheltered cove, ideal as a harbour for sailing boats, though trading ships have today been replaced by leisure craft.

Past Brawdy airfield, the route again descends to the sea. But this time, it's a far call from the protection of Solva's intimate harbour. At Newgale the full force of the wind is positively sought. This is one of Wales' most popular beaches, for the surf as much as the sand, and there is plenty of both. The route enjoys only a short rendezvous with the Atlantic spray, preferring to climb back once again to the safety of the hinterland. Through Simpson's Cross, home to the Pembrokeshire Motor Museum, and the houses of Haverfordwest appear on the horizon.

Haverfordwest to Fishguard
Haverfordwest owes its importance to its position at the highest tidal reach on the Western Cleddau. It was also the lowest feasible fording place and it was in the town that Henry Tudor crossed the river on his way from landing at Angle in 1485. His subsequent victory over Richard III at Bosworth Field gained him the crown and he became King Henry VII. The castle was originally built in the twelfth century and has faced attack by Llewelyn the Great in 1215 and the French allies of Owain Glyndŵr in 1405. Though in ruins, it still watches over the town.

Today Haverfordwest is a busy market and shopping centre, as well as being the administrative headquarters for the county.

Leaving Pembrokeshire's county town, you pass the hospital and then Withybush aerodrome. The airfield is also the site for the county's annual agricultural show in August. Open country offers prospects of the distant Preseli Mountains but soon the road crosses the Western Cleddau and enters **Treffgarne Gorge**, in the company of the river and the railway. The Cleddau has carved this pretty wooded ravine through rock. Nant-y-Coy Mill occupies a picturesque spot just below the Great Treffgarne Rocks. The mill is water powered and nature trails explore the grounds. A small museum, tea shop and craft centre are also sited here. At Wolf's Castle the road deserts the valley for the higher ground once again. Some substantial deviations from the main road serve the villages Letterston and Trecwn and just before Scleddau, the Cleddau, now an infant watercourse, is crossed once again. Its source lies just two miles from the northern coast of Pembrokeshire. After Scleddau, the vista of the sea opens up and the port of Goodwick lies ahead. You have completed a tour of western Pembrokeshire as you return to Fishguard.

Route Information

Section	Bus No.	Operator	Weekday frequency	Sunday frequency	Jny Time	Rover tickets
Cardigan - Fishguard - Haverfordwest	412	Richards Bros	Hourly	2 journeys	1 hour 15 min	FPS WW
Fishguard - St David's - Haverfordwest	411	Richards Bros	Every 2 hours (Hrly St D - H'west)	4 journeys (St D - Hwest only)	1 hour 45 min	FPS WW

Places of Interest

Cilgerran Castle, near Cardigan   01239-615007
www.cadw.wales.gov.uk

St Dogmael's Abbey, Cardigan   01443-336000
www.cadw.wales.gov.uk

Castell Henllys Iron Age Fort   01239-891319
www.castellhenllys.com

St David's Cathedral   01437-720691
www.stdavidscathdral.org.uk

St David's Bishop's Palace   01437-720517
www.cadw.wales.gov.uk

Pembrokeshire Motor Museum, near Haverfordwest
01437-710950
www.pembsmotormuseum.co.uk

Nant y Coy Mill and Museum, Treffgarne   01437-741671

Ideas for Walking
The Pembrokeshire Coast Long Distance Footpath passes near this route for most of the way. It is possible to use the excellent coastal bus services operated by the national park to create a linear walk along most sections of the path. For example, you can walk the nine mile section from the National Park Information Centre in St David's to Whitesands Bay, an outstanding cliff top walk passing the most westerly point of mainland Wales. You can return by 'Celtic Coaster' bus from Whitesands, or two intermediate points. The service runs during the summer

months and is at least hourly.

Refreshments

St David's city is a charming place and the history and atmosphere will captivate you. The smallest city in Britain also offers a variety of places to eat in restaurants, pubs and take aways.

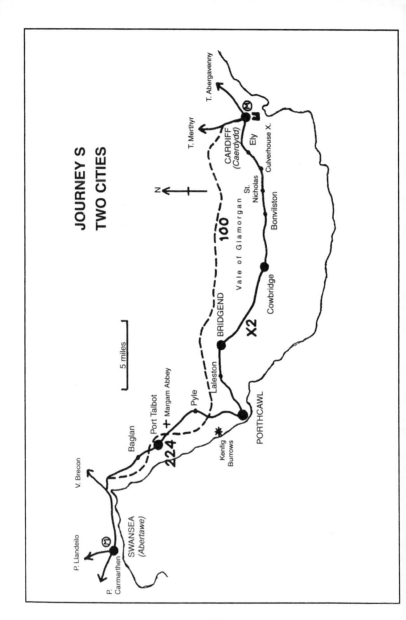

Journey S: Two Cities

Cardiff – Porthcawl - Swansea

Train or bus can complete the journey between the capital of Wales and the country's second city quickly and smoothly. The two cities are about 40 miles apart and are linked by a regular express rail service originating in London and a frequent bus service. In fact, both modes of transport are run by the same parent company. The 'Shuttle' bus service between Cardiff and Swansea runs along the M4 motorway for most of the way. It is relatively fast, though trains are much quicker and other bus routes more interesting.

If you want a more leisurely transit across the Vale of Glamorgan, try combining the two bus services described here. The first ride heads out of Cardiff across the prosperous and fertile Vale of Glamorgan, through the market town of Cowbridge, before arriving at Porthcawl, seaside playground for the valleys. The onward journey to Swansea skirts an internationally important dune system, while mountains rise up steeply from the coast. Port Talbot makes good use of this narrow coastal strip, the houses and chimneys of the town contrast starkly with the tree-clad slopes of Margam Forest. As you near the destination, the great sweep of Swansea Bay offers entrancing views of Gower and beyond.

Cardiff to Porthcawl

Cardiff is Wales' capital and largest city. All these titles are relatively recent. Cardiff was little more than a village at the start of the nineteenth century. It became the country's capital in 1955 and remains Europe's youngest capital city. Cardiff only gained its charter as a city in 1905. The development of the coal industry was the catalyst to

Cardiff's rapid expansion. The town offered an outlet to the sea for the coalfields, especially after the First Marquis of Bute built Bute West Dock. By 1900, the city handled over 10m tons of coal each year and its population had swelled to nearly 200,000. The decline of the industrial wealth of the valleys hastened the demise of the dockland areas of the city. But in the past few years a major transformation has taken place following construction of a barrage across Cardiff Bay. The waterfront is a leisure attraction and the location of some important buildings including a new opera house and the permanent home of the National Assembly. In the heart of the city centre Cardiff Castle stands as an ancient fortress restored as a mansion for the Bute family. But the city's most recent shrine is the magnificent Millennium Stadium overlooking the banks of the Taff and casting its immense shadow over the very heart of the capital.

It's a long trawl through the relentless western suburbs of Canton and Ely before the twenty-first century equivalent of city walls, a retail park, marks the boundary of the city. A steep wooded ridge lies ahead, crowned by the Wenvoe television mast and it's a steady climb up through the woods. Once at the top, the road undulates through rolling, agricultural countryside and the villages of St Nicholas and Bonvilston. This is some of the best farming land in Wales and the market town of **Cowbridge** has a distinct air of relaxed affluence. The town's council fought the arrival of the railway and so the line avoids Cowbridge, running instead through Pontyclun, some miles to the north. Iolo Morgannwg, alias Edward Williams (1747-1846) was a native of the town and is remembered for introducing the Convocation of Bards to the National Eisteddfod. His energy was not wholly honourable, reviving interest in the poet Dafydd ap Gwilym by forging medieval poetry.

The road is fast to **Bridgend**, a busy centre and focus for the Vale of Glamorgan. Over past decades this part of Wales has attracted high-tech and engineering jobs. Despite some closures, the town exudes an sense of prosperity. The ruined gateway of the Norman fort, called Newcastle, can still be seen.

The bus continues west through the village of Laleston but then leaves the main road for its final five miles into **Porthcawl**. It weaves a route through the town's suburbs before arriving at Coney Beach, playground for generations of day-trippers and holidaymakers from the industrial valleys. To the south lie the ecologically important dunes of Merthyr Mawr, part of a vast dune system that spreads most of the way along the Glamorgan coast. Across the water lie the hills of Exmoor, clearly visible on a reasonable day. Porthcawl's town centre is unremarkable with the usual small town chain store names. But its atmosphere is almost intimate. The whole of southern Wales mingles here, as if the egalitarian spirit of nonconformity has spilled out of the valleys to colonise the coast. Old ladies on the bus from Tonypandy, families with pushchairs from Aberdare, teenagers from Bridgend, the early imbiber who's forgotten the name of his home town.

Porthcawl to Swansea

From Porthcawl, the bus heads northwest towards Pyle. Although this is an agricultural area, most of the villages include extensive new housing developments, reflecting a desire for rural life, or perhaps a desire for suburban life in a rural setting. Just to the east of the road, Margam Country Park incorporates the ruins of the richest Cistercian abbey in Wales dating back to the twelfth century. Nearby are a mock Tudor mansion and the largest orangery in Britain. Margam steel works sit astride the sand dunes between here and the sea, while the terraced housing of Tai-bach huddles along the road below the hills now encroaching steeply from the east. Palm trees assert the tropical tendencies of this south-facing coast and soon the road flies over the station and market to land in Port Talbot bus station.

Port Talbot is named after Christopher Rice Talbot who financed a floating dock in 1834 to serve the mineral industries inland. The town is constricted by the sea and an abrupt mountain escarpment that forces everything into a narrow coastal corridor. The vast steel works and a chemical complex mingle with the seaside attractions of Aberavon beach.

It's a slight climb to Baglan, and this modest ascent is rewarded by excellent views across the curve of Swansea Bay to Mumbles and southwards to Devon. A viaduct carries the road across the tidal river Neath, with the motorway striding across its flyover alongside. Once over the river, a left turn abandons the company of the M4 and heads directly for **Swansea**. Crymyln Burrows lie to the south of the road, which passes the docks to arrive at the banks of the river Tawe. It's an abrupt and impressive entry into the city as you cross the river. The redeveloped marina lies down river to the south, the Victorian civic buildings skirt the road and the commercial heart of Swansea lies just ahead of you. *(More about Swansea in Journey P.)*

Route Information

Section	Bus No.	Operator	Weekday frequency	Sunday frequency	Jny Time (min)	Rover tickets
Cardiff - Porthcawl	X2	First Cymru	Every 30 min	Hourly	90	FPS
Porthcawl - Swansea	224	First Cymru	Hourly	No service*	85	FPS
Cardiff - Swansea Shuttle	100	First Cymru	Every 30 min	5 journeys*	60	FPS

NOTES
* You can return to Bridgend on route X2 and then catch the X1 to Swansea (4 journeys on a Sunday)

Places to Visit

Cardiff Castle   029-2087 8100
www.cardiff.gov.uk/castle

National Museum and Art Gallery   029-2039 7951
www.nmgw.ac.uk

Cardiff Bay Visitor Centre   029-2046 3833

Millennium Stadium (Guided Tours)   029-2082 2228
www.millenniumstadium.com

National History Museum, St Fagan's, Cardiff
029-2057 3500
www.nmgw.ac.uk

Margam Country Park   01639-881635
www.neath-porttalbot.gov

National Waterfront Museum, Swansea   01792-459640
www.waterfrontmuseum.co.uk

Dylan Thomas Centre, Swansea   01792-463980
www.dylanthomas.org

Swansea Museum   01792-653763
www.swansea.gov.uk

Singleton Park & Botanical Gardens, Swansea
01792-280210

Plantasia, Swansea   01792-474555
www.plantasia.org

Ideas for Walking
Try a city walk, exploring some of the sights of Swansea or Cardiff. Suggestions are available from either city's tourist information centre. Guided walks or self-guided trails offer an insight into history and culture that can often be missed.

Refreshments
Of course both Cardiff and Swansea offer the full range of places to eat. But don't underrate the exhilaration of fish and chips by the sea at Porthcawl.

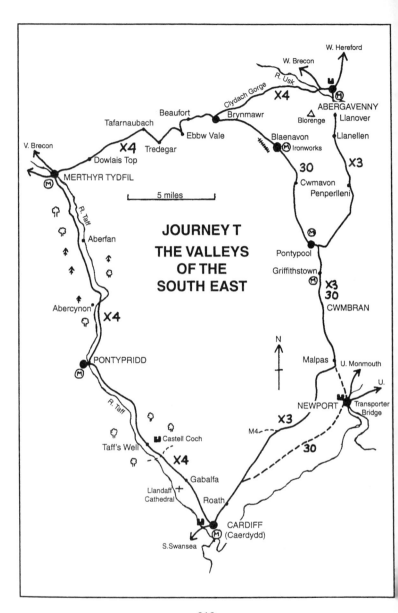

Journey T: The Valleys of the South East

Cardiff – Merthyr – Abergavenny – Cardiff

This interesting tour of the south-east's valleys includes dramatic scenery as well as a powerful heritage. It has become a cliché to say that the valleys have become green. But it is no less true for that. The circuit climbs from Wales' capital to the place that was once its largest town and then on to the country's only 'new' town. On the way, it visits the hometown of the architect of the National Health Service, the cradle of Wales' industrial revolution, and the most popular market in Wales.

Cardiff to Merthyr

On a normal day, your bus will start from **Cardiff**'s central bus station, in the shadow of the city's modern megalith, the Millennium Stadium. On serious match days, city streets are closed to traffic and northbound buses start from Greyfriars Road, just by the castle. Cardiff's castle is an iconic representation of its history from ancient times through to the industrial revolution. Originally the site was a Roman fort guarding the road between Caerleon and Carmarthen as it crossed the Taff. Later the Normans built a castle here. But it was industrial muscle rather than military might that decided its future in the eighteenth century. The first Marquis of Bute bought the castle and converted it into a luxury mansion. The Bute family were responsible for the development of Cardiff as a coal port and were principle architects of the city's Victorian prosperity.

Following the tide of traffic past the castle, you soon pass Cardiff's imposing civic quarter. The purpose built campus in **Cathays Park** on the leafy northern fringe of the city centre includes the law courts, civic centre, university buildings and National Museum and Art Gallery. On the opposite side of the road is Bute Park, only open to the public since 1947, a green lung reaching right into the heart of the city. The road north is one of the busiest roads out of the capital, taking much of the traffic towards the valleys through its northern suburbs. The top of the Gabalfa flyover affords a glimpse of Llandaff Cathedral to the west and the vast bulk of the University teaching hospital to the east. A faster dual carriageway leads across the motorway and into the Taff valley.

The Taff is the longest of the south's industrial valleys, reaching from the heart of the Brecon Beacons into the centre of the capital city. It is fed by a number of tributaries, notably the Rhondda and Cynon. North of Taff's Well, the river has driven a gorge through rock, flanked by precipitous wooded cliffs. The road, railway and river jostle for position as they snake through the narrow defile. Up to the east, **Castell Coch**, a mock fairy tale chateau straight from the Bavarian Black Forest, guards the gateway from the valleys. But this is a temple to money rather than a military fortress. It was built from 1875 as another Bute family home, this time for the third Marquis of Bute, owner of Cardiff's docks. Conical towers cling to the steep wooded buttresses and the designer, William Bruges, even included a working portcullis. Today, Cadw's stewardship means it is open to visitors.

In **Pontypridd**, the Rhondda and Taff valleys converge. 'Ponty' is one of the key towns in the valleys and has a considerable musical pedigree. It was home to Evan and James James who composed the national anthem, 'Mae hen wlad fy nhadau' ('Land of my fathers') and more recently to singer Tom Jones. Dr William Price became famous during the nineteenth century when he arranged the cremation of his baby son. He was tried for the 'crime' but the event marked the beginning of cremation's legalisation in the UK. The railway station was once hub of a great network with 500 trains a day, while the town's old bridge dates from the eighteenth century.

Above Pontypridd there is a steady ascent up the Taff valley. The Cynon valley diverges at Abercynon, bringing the waters down from the hills around Aberdare. As the road climbs towards Merthyr Vale, views of the Brecon Beacons open out with the distinctive flattened summits triumphing above the heads of the industrial valleys. Many of the scars of coal mining have disappeared, the combined work of reclamation and natural regeneration. Emotional scars still remain. The road passes across the hillside above Aberfan where, on 21st October 1966, an unstable coal tip engulfed the local primary school killing 144, including 116 children.

The road into **Merthyr** drops down to the valley floor, passing various industrial units, including the Hoover factory. Merthyr is the largest of the 'heads of the valleys' communities, and at the height of the industrial revolution was the largest town in Wales. *(For more details on Merthyr see Journey V.)*

Merthyr to Abergavenny

It's a long climb out of the Taff valley. Predictably the bus takes the old road through Penydarren, passing a monument in the form of a steam engine. It commemorates Richard Trevethick, a Cornish engineer, who was the first person to run a steam train service in the world. On 21st February 1804 he ran an engine from

Merthyr to Abercynon carrying 10 tons of iron and 70 unofficial passengers. Trevethick effectively invented the steam engine, but its exploitation was left to George Stevenson to whom history has given the recognition. Along the road seedy but impressive Victorian buildings are interspersed with more humble housing and derelict spaces. The townscape witnesses to a proud industrial past but also to the struggle with poverty and unemployment today. The road has climbed 200 metres in height by the time it reaches **Dowlais Top**, where a retail park and hypermarket perch on a squelchy bog nearly 400 metres above sea level.

The Heads of the Valleys road was built in the 1960s to connect the communities at the top of the industrial valleys. In its day it was a considerable feat of engineering with viaducts, cuttings and graded ascents. The bus follows the road for a while but then leaves it to serve **Tredegar**, at the head of the Sirhowy valley. The town is best known as home to Aneurin Bevan (1897-1960), Labour MP and founder of the National Health Service. The next valley cradles **Ebbw Vale**. A massive steel works was built here in 1938 but lasted just 40 years. Decline of coal and steel have taken a toll, but great energy has always held out the prospect of revival and regeneration. The steel works site became a garden festival in 1992 and the heart of it remains open to visitors.

The highest point of the Heads of the Valleys road is reached between Ebbw Vale and Brynmawr, though the bus sticks to the urban route through Beaufort to reach Brynmawr. From Brynmawr the bus to Abergavenny drops steadily down the **Clydach Gorge**. The steep sided ravine offers insights into the early industrial revolution. The road threads its way down between rocky cuttings clad with shrubs and trees, hiding evidence of early iron making. Iron was smelted here from the seventeenth century and limestone quarried. There is a perceptible scenic and cultural shift as the Usk valley is approached. In place of the gritty industrial heritage of the mountains, the fertile agricultural land of the vale has always yielded wealth and prosperity, at least for some. The bus serves the communities of Gilwern and Govilon before crossing the Usk and passing Neville Hall Hospital into the thriving market town of Abergavenny.

Abergavenny to Cardiff

Every Tuesday, visitors and traders from a wide area of Wales and neighbouring counties of England swamp **Abergavenny**. They come, many on special 'Tuesdays Only' buses, to Abergavenny market. The importance and success of the market indicates the strategic position of Abergavenny, gateway into the hinterland of Wales and trading centre for a wide rural area. Most of the townscape is Georgian or Victorian, though some clues to its greater antiquity remain. There are a few remains of the castle, dating from 1090 and the Parish Church, once a priory, still includes a Norman font. The town guards the upper reaches of the Usk valley and is surrounded by three hills, the Sugar Loaf to the northwest, Ysgyryd Fawr to the northeast and the Blorenge to the south.

It is through this pastoral, agricultural country that the first part of the journey to Cardiff begins. Passing though Llanover, the road more or less follows the line of the **Monmouthshire and Brecon Canal**. Iron was brought down the side of the Blorenge on inclines and shipped to Newport from wharves along the canal. Remains of such a quay can be seen at Goytre Wharf. At **Pontypool**, we join the valley of the Afon Lwyd, locally known as the

223

Eastern Valley. The bus leaves the main road to serve the town. Tinplate was brought to Pontypool from Germany in 1730 and established the town as a key iron-making centre. The town's japanned-ware teapots, plates and trays were world famous. Pontypool Park, now an extensive public park, was originally the home of ironmaster, John Hanbury.

The bus needs passengers and so chooses the urban, western side of the valley, serving Griffithstown and Sebastopol, eventually arriving at the centre of Wales' only new town, **Cwmbrân**. Established after the Second World War, the town is now the sixth largest place in the country, overshadowing the other communities in the Eastern Valley. Our bus now heads directly and speedily for Cardiff. Fast roads lead to Malpas, where the M4 is joined. The motorway by passes Newport and soon approaches the fringes of Cardiff. A series of dual carriageways and flyovers avoids the tortuous monotony of suburbia bringing you directly across the Rumney marshes and into Cardiff.

Alternative route exploring Blaenavon World Heritage Site

Between Brynmawr and Pontypool, an interesting alternative route explores the upper reaches of the Eastern Valley and the world heritage site at Blaenavon. An hourly bus service runs from Brynmawr through Blaenavon to Pontypool, Cwmbrân and Newport. (There are more frequent services south of Blaenavon). You can connect into the Cardiff service at either Pontypool or Cwmbrân.

Blaenavon was declared a world heritage site in 2000, one of only about 20 such locations in Britain. The reason is its pivotal role in the development of iron production. The Blorenge is riddled with important archaeological remains and this area can rightly lay claim to be the cradle of the industrial revolution in Wales. Alexander Cordell's historical novel, 'Rape of the Fair Country', is set in nineteenth century industrial Monmouthshire and features many places around the town. In Blaenavon, you can visit the old ironworks, now in the care of Cadw. The site includes ironworkers' cottages. The national coalmining museum of Wales is on the lower slopes of the Coity Mountain at Big Pit and offers trips underground. There is also a preserved steam railway, running on part of the line that served the upper reaches of the Eastern Valley. A number of second hand bookshops have opened in the town in an attempt to emulate the success of Hay-on-Wye.

South of Blaenavon, the bus climbs through Varteg and winds down through Garndiffaith and Abersychan. One of the largest cave systems in Britain was recently discovered in Pontnewynydd. You can rejoin the main route at either Pontypool or Cwmbrân.

Route Information

Section	Bus No.	Operator	Weekday frequency	Sunday frequency	Jny Time	Rover tickets
Cardiff - Merthyr -	X4	Stagecoach	Every 30	No service	2 hours	FPS
Brynmawr - Abergavenny *		in S Wales	min		20 min	NR
Abergavenny - Pontypool - Cwmbrân - Cardiff*	X3	Stagecoach in S Wales	Hourly	No service	1 hour 30 min	FPS NR
Brynmawr - Blaenavon - Cwmbrân**	30	Stagecoach in S Wales	Hourly	No service	1 hour 20 min	FPS NR
NOTES						
*Services extend to/from Hereford every 2 hours (See Journey X) ** Service continues to Newport. Other services available between Blaenavon and Cwmbrân, giving several buses an hour.						

Places to visit

Cardiff Castle   029-2087 8100
                         www.cardiff.gov.uk/castle

National Museum and Art Gallery   029-2039 7951
                                www.nmgw.ac.uk

Cardiff Bay Visitor Centre   029-2046 3833

Millennium Stadium (Guided Tours)   029-2082 2228
                         www.millenniumstadium.com

National History Museum,
St Fagan's, Cardiff   029-2057 3500
                                www.nmgw.ac.uk

Castell Coch, Taff's Well   029-2081 0101
                         www.cadw.wales.gov.uk

Cyfarthfa Castle, Merthyr   01685-723112
                         www.museums.merthyr.gov.uk

Joseph Parry's Cottage, Merthyr   01685-383704
                         www.museums.merthyr.gov.uk

Brecon Mountain Railway, Pant, Merthyr   01685-722988
                         www.breconmountainrailway.co.uk

Blaenavon Ironworks   01495-792615
                         www.cadw.wales.gov.uk

Big Pit National Coal Museum, Blaenavon

01495-790311

www.nmgw.ac.uk

Pontypool and Blaenavon Railway, Blaenavon

01495-792263

www.pontypool-and-blaenavon.co.uk

Abergavenny Museum   01873-854282

www.monmouthshire.gov

Pontypool Museum   01495-752036

www.pontypoolmuseum.org.uk

Griffithstown Railway Museum   01495-762908

Ideas for Walking

The Taff Trail is a 55-mile waymarked route for walkers and cyclists from Brecon to Cardiff. It cuts through the heart of the Brecon Beacons on the track of an old railway and then descends the Taff Valley from Merthyr. Good local buses and trains on the southern section make it easy to walk a shorter section, making use of public transport. For more information, telephone 0800 243731.

Refreshments

You could pause for refreshments at any of the change points on this circuit. Cwmbrân's town centre is an under cover shopping mall that includes restaurants and pubs. Merthyr and Abergavenny both have a full range of facilities, the latter being especially busy on Tuesday for the market.

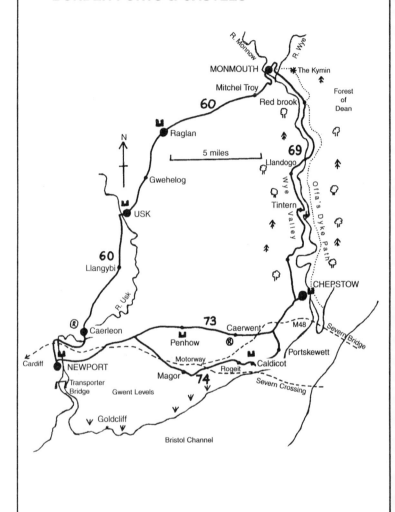

JOURNEY U
BORDER FORTS & CASTLES

R. Monnow

R. Wye

MONMOUTH   ✳ The Kymin

Mitchel Troy

Forest
of
Dean

60

Red brook

Raglan

N

5 miles

69

Llandogo

Gwehelog

Wye Valley

Tintern

Offa's Dyke Path

USK

60

Llangybi

R. Usk

CHEPSTOW

Ⓡ

Caerleon

73

Caerwent

M48

Severn Bridge

Penhow

Ⓡ

Portskewett

Motorway

Caldicot

Cardiff

NEWPORT

Magor

Rogeit

74

Transporter
Bridge

Gwent Levels

Severn Crossing

Goldcliff

Bristol Channel

Journey U: Forts and Castles in Border Country

Monmouth – Chepstow – Newport – Monmouth

No fewer than seven castles and five Roman settlements on this route reveal the strategic importance of the rolling hills of Gwent. In Roman times, this was the country of the Silures, the fiercest and most feared of all British tribes. Medieval castles bear witness to the significance of the county in a later era, guarding the approaches to Wales across the Severn and Wye. But today, tumbling streams and farm animals contribute the majority of noise in the peaceful, wooded hills and rich agricultural land of Monmouthshire. The southern section of the route crosses through the busier commuter land between Chepstow and Newport and gives you a glimpse of the commercial and industrial importance of S Wales, past and present. Even here, the low-lying Gwent levels are a haven for ornithologists and reveal what may have been a seventeenth century tsunami.

Monmouth to Chepstow

Monmouth is a border town. Just three miles away is the Royal Forest of Dean and in the shops of Monnow Street you will hear the burr of the Gloucestershire dialect as well as the flattened vowels of south-east England and, of course, the homegrown lilt of Gwent. Monmouth has nearly always been prosperous, despite periods of crisis such as the Black Death and periodic flooding from its two rivers.

The Romans founded a garrison here and called it Blestium; archaeologists have found evidence of their occupation. In the eleventh century, the Normans were quick to occupy the area and a castle was built on a rock between the Wye and Monnow. In the thirteenth century, a fortified river crossing was built as a gateway into the town. The only one of its kind in Britain, the Monnow Bridge is still complete today and has only recently enjoyed a belated retirement as the main road entry into the town centre from the west.

The bus station is situated at this lower end of the town, close to the bridge. Our journey begins by ascending the broad sweep of Monnow Street towards the slender spire of the Parish Church. On the right at the top of the street you can see the Shire Hall, built in 1724. In front is a statue of Henry V, victor of Agincourt, who was born in the castle in 1387. The square in front of the Hall bears the name of the famous victory over the French, immortalised by Shakespeare. Also in front of the Shire Hall is a statue of Charles Stewart Rolls, also born in Monmouth. Co-founder of Rolls Royce, he is shown admiring a model of an early aeroplane and he himself was a keen aviator, laying claim to the first non-stop return trip across the channel. His enthusiasm proved fatal as he was killed in an accident on the south coast of England in 1910. Rolls also brought the first motorcar to Monmouth, taking three days to drive from Cambridge while an undergraduate there. The Shire Hall was also venue for the trial' of John Frost and the leaders of the Chartist rebellion in 1839, their death sentences commuted to transportation to the colonies. More about the Chartists later.

Passing the Parish Church, the bus travels right through to the northern end of the town before turning back to follow the dual carriageway by-pass and turning left to cross the Wye. Nelson visited Monmouth in 1802. He supported the building of a 'naval temple' to commemorate sixteen admirals and their exploits in the eighteenth century, again at the expense of Britain's nearest continental neighbours. The 'temple' is built high up on the ridge above the eastern bank of the Wye, known as the Kymin. The Round House here is a curious white circular building dating from 1794, which stands out on the top of the hill. It was built as the focus for a bowling green for the gentlemen of Monmouth. Owned by the National Trust, the Kymin still supports pleasant woodland walks with outstanding views over Monmouth. It's also a good pause on Offa's Dyke footpath before beginning the descent into the Wye Valley.

Enjoy the scenic beauty of the Wye Valley as the river follows its final course from Pumlumon near Aberystwyth. Its passage through limestone and sandstone hills offers an unrivalled sylvan journey. The border joins the river at Redbrook and the route lies on the English side until Bigsweir Bridge, then passes through Llandogo to arrive at Tintern.

Tintern Abbey is the best-preserved medieval abbey in Wales. Founded in 1131 by Cistercian monks, it escaped the worst of medieval instability through being tucked away from the more contentious regions of Wales. It did not, however, escape the dissolution of the monasteries by Henry VIII in 1536. But it's not so much the exemplary Gothic architecture, as its natural amphitheatre that gives Tintern evocative charm. Here is one of Wales' original tourist attractions. Wordsworth wrote a poem about it, Turner painted it. According to an undated legend, a group of young men decided to excavate the precincts one day. They discovered the remains of two bodies and celebrated their find with open-air revels. During the evening a thunderstorm interrupted the proceedings and the youths were horrified to see the figure of a knight clad in armour surrounded by the ghostly spectre of hooded monks. Apparently they had disturbed the rest of the Earl of Pembroke, known as 'Strongbow'. As the knight appeared to raise his sword, the young men fled in instant sobriety. Tintern is now in the care of Cadw and is well worth a visit.

Leaving Tintern, the bus soon climbs out of the Wye Valley through the village of St Arvan's and past Chepstow racecourse. On the opposite bank you can see the 70 metre high limestone cliffs of Wintour's Leap, now a favourite spot for rock climbers. The cliff is named after Sir John Wintour, who apparently leapt off the cliff on horseback and swam across the river to avoid capture by the Roundheads in the Civil War. A short descent brings us to the ancient border stronghold of Chepstow.

Chepstow to Newport

Chepstow, a historic walled frontier town, guards the entrance to southern Wales in a spectacular setting at the lower end of a dramatic limestone gorge. Chepstow Castle occupies the whole length of the cliffs on the Welsh side of the Wye, commanding the crossing from England. In a land of castles, this one is special. It is probably the oldest stone castle in Britain, certainly in Wales. Its strategic importance was such that William fitz Osbern chose a permanent construction when other early Norman castles were still wooden motte and bailey fortifications. Its walls appear to rise seamlessly out of the mellow cliffs on which they are built, looking over the swirling tidal waters of the river below. The castle was extended and rebuilt over the medieval period, giving a good insight into the development of castles. It endured two sieges in the Civil War when a new frontier between Royalist Gwent and Parliamentarian Gloucestershire became paramount. The castle was maintained until 1690, but then fell into disrepair. However, today it has endured well and there is plenty to see.

Chepstow's thirteenth century town (or port) walls still remind the visitor of the town's maritime past. Much of the town's wealth came from shipbuilding in the seventeenth and eighteenth centuries and the Georgian buildings climbing up the steep streets evidence this.

You have a choice of routes from Chepstow to Newport.

Bus 74 winds through the flatter, coastal area, serving a variety of communities that have emerged and grown over the past 50 years. Climbing out of Chepstow, it then descends Pwllmeyric hill and turns left to leave the A48. There is a good panorama of both Severn crossings as the bus approaches Portskewett. A ribbon of urban development lies most of the way from here to Magor, encouraged by easy access to Bristol. Until 1966, the only land route to southern England was via Gloucester. In that year the ferry from Beachley to Aust was gracefully retired as the Queen opened the Severn Bridge. A second crossing was opened in the 1990s carrying the M4 directly across to Magor. The proximity of the Bristol Channel, and its shipping, did not escape the notice of the Normans, who built a motte and bailey castle at Calidicot in 1086. This was subsequently rebuilt of stone and enlarged during several periods in its colourful history. In the nineteenth century a notorious antiquary, JR Cobb, acquired it and used it as a family home. Now owned by Monmouthshire County Council and set in 55 acres of country park, it invites exploration.

The **Gwent levels** comprise low-lying marshes

233

between the Wye and Rhymney estuaries. These levels include reens, salt marsh and coastal turf and offer important habitats for birds, plants and invertebrates. Local people are used to the phenomenon of the Severn bore, which is created by funnelling high tides through the Bristol Channel into the narrower and shallower Severn estuary. However, in 2005 a researcher at Bath Spa University College, Dr Simon Haslett, concluded that a tsunami had hit the coastal areas of Gwent and Somerset. Evidence from archaeology and local records was used to support the claim that a wave inundated the low-lying land of the Gwent levels on 30th January 1607. The wave reached up to 4 miles inland, travelled up to 38mph and reached a height of 7.5 metres. One local source records that a wealthy women, Mistress Van, lived four miles from the sea near Newport and although she saw the wave approaching from her house she could not get upstairs before it rushed through and drowned her. The wave is recorded in various local churches, including Goldcliff.

After Magor the country becomes more rural though you have a good glimpse of the Llanwern steel works, built in the 1960s as an attempt to boost the economy of SE Wales.

The alternative route from Chepstow, taken by Bus 73, follows the A48 through **Caerwent** and Penhow. The Romans established Caerwent as a market town called Venta Silurum, market of the Silures. Originally built of timber, it was later laid out on a conventional grid pattern with stone buildings. Today the village boasts some of the finest remains of Roman walls, and other remnants include a row of shops and a house. Moving towards Newport, the village of **Penhow** contains one of the oldest inhabited castles in Wales. Originally a Norman fortress, it is now open to the public. You can visit the twelfth century battlements and the fifteenth century Great Hall, complete with minstrels' gallery, aided by a walkman tour. George Borrow travelled along the route of the A48 as he finished his marathon walking tour of Wales in 1854. Although this is border country, a conversation between Borrow and a stranger in Newport revealed that the Welsh language was alive and well eight miles east of the town in that year. Although the oldest European language suffered decline in the years that followed, there is a revival of Welsh right across SE Wales today with many courses well subscribed and Welsh medium schools thriving.

The two routes converge at Langstone, as we begin the approach to Newport. The provision of at least four major hotels by the M4 junction must make this a particularly favoured spot for overnight stays! As you near the centre of Newport watch out for the Transporter Bridge, which was opened in 1906. The bridge carries people and vehicles over the river on an aerial gondola, suspended from the 54m high centre span. The rapid development of Newport at the end of the nineteenth century created the need for a crossing over the dangerous tidal flows of the Usk estuary. Originally built to avoid disruption to shipping, the bridge has been recently restored and is one of only two such structures in Britain. A visitor centre interprets its history. On our route, however, the Usk is crossed by Newport Bridge, passing the fourteenth century castle on the right.

Newport to Monmouth

Having recently gained city status, **Newport** is the third largest place in Wales. The lowest crossing of the Usk has been a key strategic location for centuries but it was only during the industrial revolution that Newport grew in importance as the iron and coal port for the eastern and western valleys of Monmouthshire. The social tensions and upheavals that accompanied this period of history became focused in the Chartist movement, which campaigned for electoral reform. It was especially strong in the valleys of SE Wales with up to 25,000 supporters. On 4th November 1839 a huge, highly motivated and idealistic group of Chartists marched on Newport. But they were badly organised and the constables were waiting for them, hidden in the Westgate Hotel at the bottom of Stow Hill. Up to 22 Chartists were killed; ten are buried in unmarked graves in St Woolos Cathedral, at the top of Stow Hill. Newport's main shopping precinct is named after one of the leaders, John Frost, who was exiled to Tasmania. The rising is commemorated by statues in Commercial Street, commissioned for the 150th anniversary of the rising in 1999. The city centre hosts a number of other statues, murals and mosaics depicting aspects of Newport's history, which deserve exploration. Also worth visiting are the Cathedral and the Art Gallery and Museum. Although parts of Newport were marred by dull concrete in the 1960s and 1970s, it remains an excellent shopping centre and a place with much history and interest.

The bus sweeps out of Newport on a dual carriageway to cross the motorway just east of the notorious Brynglas tunnels and then leaves through the suburbs of the city to reach the Roman fortress of **Caerleon**. In AD 75, the Romans established a fortress here at the lowest crossing point of the Usk. Beside the military garrison there was also a substantial town. This combination has bequeathed us what is undoubtedly the best collection of Roman remains in Britain. You can view the bathhouse, the barracks and one of the best-preserved amphitheatres in the world. There is also a museum and visitor centre. Later, King Arthur held his court here. Geoffrey of Monmouth wrote around 1133 that at Whitsun, Arthur 'made up his mind to hold a plenary court at that season and place the crown of the kingdom on his head…in the City of the Legions.' Legends allege that Caerleon was the mythical seat of Camelot, though the evidence for this is more imaginative than convincing. The myths and history have drawn people through the ages and Alfred Lord Tennyson stayed in the Hanbury Arms, by the bridge, while writing the Idylls of the King in 1856. Recently, some of the original wooden bridge that spanned the Usk until the early nineteenth century has been discovered in excavation.

Leaving Caerleon, the bus follows the original main road through Llangybi to Usk. The countryside is undulating, pleasant and rich in agriculture. **Usk** is a charming small town on the banks of its namesake river. It is believed that the Norman town and castle were founded in 1120, itself built on the site of a Roman fort. The castle is open daily, except Christmas Day, in return for a small donation. In the centre of the town lies Twyn Square, centred round a Victorian clock. The town is also home to the Gwent Rural Life Museum, housed in an old malt barn. Run by volunteers, displays trace the history of the county from Victorian times, illustrated by many exhibits.

Five miles beyond Usk lies the historic village of **Raglan**, dominated by its castle which still today marks the place where routes to south and west Wales part. Although there may have been a Norman mound here, the present ruins date from about 1430, making Raglan the last of the great Welsh castles. It saw real conflict only in 1546 when it was besieged by Parliamentary troops and nearly destroyed. Much still remains, including the Yellow Tower of Gwent and some of the magnificent Tudor gardens.

The final leg of the bus route continues through the rolling pastures of Monmouthshire, with wooded hills rising up either side of the Trothy valley. Through and around villages such as Dingestow and Mitchel Troy, your journey concludes by crossing the ancient Monnow Bridge to return to your starting point.

Route Information

Section	Bus No.	Operator	Weekday frequency	Sunday frequency	Jny Time (min)	Rover tickets
Monmouth - Chepstow	69	Chepstow Classic Coaches	Every 2 hrs	2 hourly	60	FPS NR
Chepstow - Newport via Caldicot	74	Stagecoach in S Wales	Hourly	2 hourly	60	FPS NR
Chepstow - Newport Via Caerwent	73	Stagecoach in S Wales	Hourly	No service	60	FPS NR
Newport - Raglan - Monmouth	60	HH Coaches	Every 2 hrs	No service	60	FPS NR
Newport - Caerleon	2	Newport Transport	Every 15 min	Every 30 min	20	FPS NR

Places to Visit

Monmouth Castle and Regimental Museum
01600-772175
www.monmouthcastlemuseum.org.uk

Nelson Museum, Monmouth   01600-713519
www.nelsonmuseum@monmouthshire.gov.uk

Tintern Abbey   01291-689251
www.cadw.wales.gov.uk

Chepstow Castle	01291-624065
	www.cadw.wales.gov.uk
Chepstow Museum	01291-625981
Caldicot Castle	01291-420241
	www.caldicotcastle.co.uk
Newport Tourist Information	01633-842962
	www.newport.gov.uk
Caerleon Roman Baths and Amphitheatre	
	01633-422518
	www.cadw.wales.gov.uk
Gwent Rural Life Museum, Usk	01291-673777
Raglan Castle	01291-690228
	www.cadw.wales.gov.uk

Ideas for Walking

The southernmost section of the 177-mile Offa's Dyke long distance footpath runs between Chepstow (or, more precisely, Sedbury Cliffs) to Monmouth. It is possible to walk this 17-mile section and return by bus. Alternatively you can pick up the bus at any point where the path approaches the road. The most convenient points are Redbrook, Bigsweir and Brockweir. There are spectacular views over the wooded Wye Valley.

Refreshments

You could make a leisurely stop at Monmouth or Chepstow. Pubs serve food in Usk, Raglan and Tintern as well as other places en route.

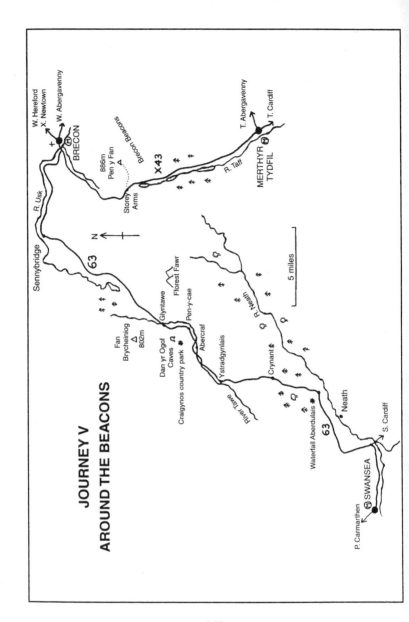

JOURNEY V
AROUND THE BEACONS

240

Journey V: The Beacons

Swansea – Brecon – Merthyr

Climbing up from Swansea Bay to the highest ground in southern Britain, this route follows the valleys of four of the great rivers of southern Wales, as they tumble down towards the coast from the wild moorland of the Brecon Beacons National Park. The three cities of the south, Cardiff, Swansea and Newport owe their importance, in part at least, to their position on the final reaches of the Taff, Tawe and Usk respectively, while the fourth river, the Neath, bequeaths the finest collection of waterfalls in Wales.

Swansea to Brecon

Don't be fooled by an undistinguished departure, lurking out of a gloomy access road on the periphery of **Swansea** Bus Station. This is a fine route that passes the highest ground in southern Britain. You will not be disappointed with the alluring grandeur of the scene from your window. But, as a prelude, don't miss some glimpses of Wales' second city.

Emerging from the Quadrant Centre, you pass a collection of Victorian civic buildings set in gardens on your right, among them Swansea Museum. Immediately afterwards, you cross the Tawe, which gives the city its indigenous name, Abertawe. Look downstream, right, to see the Millennium Bridge and newly regenerated Maritime Quarter. Swansea has a proud industrial past and, along with many such areas, it endured and battled against decline and decay as old industries were superseded. But the waterfront renewal and many other projects bear witness to the city's energy and self-belief.

The old dock, closed in 1969, has now been reborn as a vibrant focus for leisure with a marina, theatre, restaurants, a hotel and new housing. The Quarter also hosts the Maritime and Industrial Museum, focusing on Swansea's transport history. Nearby, in the old Guildhall, is the Dylan Thomas Centre, the national centre for literature in Wales, with exhibitions on the life of one of Swansea's most famous inhabitants.

No whim or chance of history can ever steal Swansea's magnificent setting on the splendid sweep of its own bay. No other British city can rival its five-mile, graciously curving promenade, decked by a series of gardens and green spaces, stretching westward towards the cliffs of Mumbles and the Gower. The city is also unique in having an entire 'area of outstanding natural beauty' within its borders. Gower was the first AONB in Britain when it was created in 1956. Behind the city, the rising terraces of decorated brick housing meet the hills and moors of mid Wales, as they roll down almost to the shores of the Bristol Channel with (weather permitting) enticing views southward to Exmoor. *(More about Swansea in Journey P.)*

Having crossed the Tawe, the bus leaves the city quickly, using Fabian Way, the main eastward route from Swansea. Crossing reclaimed marshes, you pass dockland areas and Swansea's main Park and Ride point to reach the M4. The motorway and its attendant slip roads leap high across the swampy estuary on a string of viaducts. After a short stretch of motorway, you branch off to join the Heads of the Valleys Road.

We are now in the Vale of Neath, bypassing its namesake town. This is one of the prettiest of the valleys. Limestone outcrops are host to woods that conceal the fast flowing streams tumbling down from the north.

Even though this is not a limited stop service, the bus's first call may well be in the village of **Aberdulais**. Copper, tin and iron have been worked here, but the works, long abandoned, now give a fascinating insight into industrial history. However it is the **Dulais Falls** that will catch the visitor's attention most today. Almost hidden by trees and vegetation, the river Dulais plunges through rocky gullies down a series of cascades. The site is now managed by the National Trust and is open to view.

The bus follows the valley of the Dulais upwards out of the Vale of Neath, though you can't see the river itself. Ascending through the delightful wooded country of Crynant Forest, it passes through the occasional small community before reaching the watershed. A steep and sinuous descent brings us back into the Swansea Valley with a younger Tawe passing through the town of **Ystradgynlais**.

The Tawe remains our companion as we trace its course towards its birthplace in the Black Mountain away to the northwest. But first enjoy the fine scenery as the road climbs through Abercraf. This is limestone country and wherever there is limestone, there are caves. So it should be no surprise to find here one of the UK's largest show caves, **Dan-yr-Ogof**. Open to the public, the caves were only discovered in 1912. Stalactites and stalagmites form fascinating features, enhanced by imaginative lighting effects, recorded commentaries and tableaux. If caves don't appeal, try the dinosaur park, the geological trail, and the museum or Iron Age farm. A dry ski-slope completes the repertoire of the Dan-yr-Ogof complex. Nearby, Craig-y-Nos Country Park includes a nineteenth century manor house, its grounds and a small museum.

After Abercraf the road climbs more in earnest through the bracken-clad hills rising either side of the valley. On the right soars the limestone massif of Fforest Fawr, while on the left the sandstone backbone of the Black Mountain leads up to Carmarthen Fan. From the road's summit, the eye is drawn towards the bold profile of this escarpment to the west. Brakes replace low gears and the broad sweep of the Usk valley lies ahead as we swap Swansea's river for Newport's. Descending through dairy country, **Sennybridge** is reached at the junction with the A40, the main route to West Wales and the port of Fishguard. Following the Usk through rich agricultural country, the bus passes the village of Llanspyddid, and soon reaches Brecon. If you're used to a bus that crawls interminably through city traffic, you may find this part of the journey surprising. It takes just 1 hour and 25 minutes to travel the 50 miles from Swansea!

Brecon to Merthyr

Brecon is an appealing town and marks the gateway into mid Wales. It's an agricultural and tourist centre, though it also has a long association with the army. The barracks guard the eastern entry to the town along the A40. There is also a small museum here. The cathedral for the diocese of Swansea and Brecon is situated on a hill just above the town centre. Originally the church of a Benedictine Priory, it became the town's parish church after the dissolution of the monasteries in the 1530s and was made a cathedral in 1923. A neighbouring sixteenth century tithe barn houses a heritage centre that interprets the history and work of the cathedral. An attractive town centre with narrow alleyways and good services make the town a good stopover point.

The journey south from here to Merthyr passes through the heart of the Brecon Beacons National Park.

About three buses a day continue to Cardiff, but all of them call at Merthyr bus and rail stations so it's easy to make onward connections in any case. As Brecon is left behind the road begins to climb alongside the Tafell, a tributary of the Usk. The country is a blend of contrasts. Lower down, a pastoral landscape of verdant hedgerows boasting rich plant life and colourful flowers in summer. Higher up, the rugged grassy sandstone slopes draw your gaze towards the highest ground in southern Britain. Mind you, this road offers the easiest platform to climb to the summit of the Beacons. From the top of the road, at **Storey Arms**, a relatively easy graded track climbs the 1,500 remaining feet to Pen-y-Fan (2960 feet), a favourite jaunt to which the multiplicity of parked cars bears witness.

Beyond the Storey Arms, the road begins to descend into the valley of the Taf Fawr as it begins its progress towards the Welsh capital. The forested slopes soon reveal Llwyn-Onn reservoir down on the right and shortly afterwards the suburbs of Merthyr begin. Past Cefn Coed you can see **Cyfarthfa Castle** a short way to the left. Now owned by Merthyr Council and open to the public, together with its park, Cyfarthfa was once the home of the Crawshay family, iron magnates of the industrial revolution. Built in 1825, it boasts 72 rooms and extensive grounds, an island of luxury amidst the turmoil and grit of the largest iron-making centre in the world at one time. Although Cyfarthfa is a 'mock' castle, the Crawshays may have felt in need of protection. To get a feel of the hardships and emotions of the ironworkers in the early nineteenth century, read 'Rape of the Fair Country', a historical novel set in nearby the Monmouthshire iron town of Blaenavon. In the mid-nineteenth century, such was the activity, that **Merthyr**

245

Tydfil was the largest town in the whole of Wales. Riots were common in the nineteenth century. In 1831, a 23-year-old miner, known as Dic Penderyn, was hanged for stabbing a soldier, despite protesting his innocence. His case still arouses emotions today. The town includes a number of other visitor attractions including Ynysfach Iron Heritage Centre and the cottage of Joseph Parry, the nineteenth century composer.

From Merthyr, you can carry on south down the Taff valley to Cardiff or climb east across the 'Heads of the Valleys' to Abergavenny *(both Journey T)*.

Route Information

!! Warning
The X43 is an amalgam of various transport needs, partly connected to the Brecon Beacons National Park. It is likely to face further change, or to be split into separate sections. Just watch out for changes of timetable, service number or operator.

Section	Bus No.	Operator	Weekday frequency	Sunday frequency	Jny Time	Rover tickets
Swansea - Brecon	63	Stagecoach in S Wales	3 journeys	No service	1 hour 25 min	FPS NR
Brecon - Merthyr*	X43	Sixty Sixty	Every 2 hours	2 journeys	40 min	FPS

NOTES
* This service currently starts in Abergavenny and some journeys continue to Cardiff but has been subject to frequent changes.

Places to Visit

National Waterfront Museum, Swansea   01792-459640
www.waterfrontmuseum.co.uk

Dylan Thomas Centre, Swansea   01792-463980
                                  www.dylanthomas.org

Swansea Museum   01792-653763
                                  www.swansea.gov.uk

Singleton Park & Botanical Gardens, Swansea
                                          01792-280210

Plantasia, Swansea   01792-474555
                                  www.plantasia.org

Maritime and Industrial Museum, Swansea
                          01792-650351/01792-463980

Dan-yr-Ogof Caves, Abercraf   01639-730284
                                  www.showcaves.co.uk

Craig-y-Nos Country Park   01639-730395

Brecon Cathedral   01874-623857

South Wales Borderers and Mon. Regt. Museum
                                          01874-613310
                                  www.rrw.org.uk

Cyfarthfa Castle, Merthyr   01685-723112
                          www.museums.merthyr.gov.uk

Joseph Parry's Cottage, Merthyr   01685-383704
                          www.museums.merthyr.gov.uk

Brecon Mountain Railway, Pant, Merthyr   01685-722988
                          www.breconmountainrailway.co.uk

Ideas for Walking

Corn Du and Pen-y-Fan (2960 feet), the two highest
Beacons, can be reached from Storey Arms on the A470
between Brecon and Merthyr. 4 mile round trip and 1,500
ft of ascent. A clear path but this is a mountain walk and
you should be properly equipped with protective
clothing, map compass and boots.

Refreshments

Pause in Brecon for a look around this historic town.
Among many places to eat is the refectory in the
Cathedral, which stands on a small hill overlooking the
town centre.

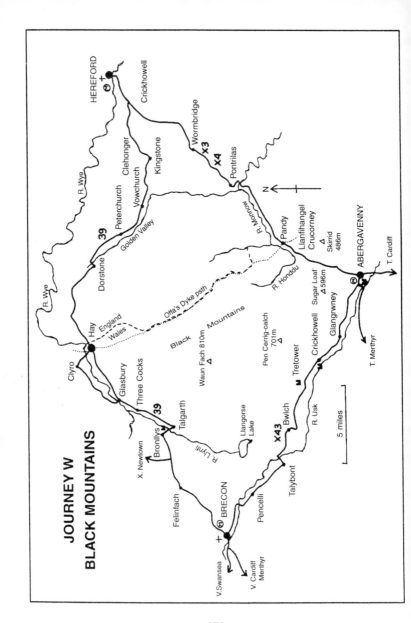

JOURNEY W
BLACK MOUNTAINS

250

Journey W: The Black Mountains

Brecon – Hay – Hereford – Abergavenny – Brecon

A circular route through some fine and varied scenery both sides of the border. It travels along the Usk and Wye valleys, visits two cathedrals and the world's most famous book town. Along the way we meet the Victorian parson whose diaries still entertain today and explore some of the most hotly disputed borderland between Wales and England. The Black Mountains are never far away and lend a touch of mystery and wildness to the rich pastoral landscape of the valleys.

Brecon to Hereford

Brecon is a historic and attractive town. It straddles the river Usk at its confluence with the Honddu, on a strategic route to western Wales. The Romans built a fort as a staging post on their road between Gloucester and Carmarthen. The Normans built a castle. Still today, Brecon is home to the South Wales Borderers, maintaining the town's military heritage through their barracks and museum. The Brecon Beacons rise to the south and their distinctive profile dominates the view *(See Journey V)*. To the north lies the wild unspoilt country of Mynydd Epynt. The main London to Fishguard trunk road passes between these mountain wildernesses, following the Usk valley westwards. In the heart of such a rural landscape, Brecon is an important agricultural centre. Its townscape includes many Georgian buildings as well as some tasteful newer developments, including the basin at the end of the Monmouthshire and Brecon Canal.

The bus out of Brecon climbs out of the town, passing

the hospital, college and leisure centre. It soon joins the main road leading from the by-pass. It's now an undulating journey through hilly country with trees dotted across the landscape. The outline of the Black Mountains lies ahead and you pass through the village of Felinfach before arriving in Bronllys. Turning off the main road here, the remains of **Bronllys Castle** are passed on the left just before a bridge over the river Llynfi. This watercourse drains Llangorse Lake, the largest natural lake in southern Wales. The castle was originally a Norman motte and bailey construction, with the stone keep added later. It features in the writings of Gerald of Wales, when writing about his trek around the country to recruit soldiers for the crusades with Baldwin, the Archbishop of Canterbury. He tells of the Earl of Hereford, Mahel, who was staying at the castle in 1165 when a fire broke out. A stone struck Mahel, who died believing it to be divine retribution for his harassment of the Bishop of St David's, incidentally Gerald's uncle.

Talgarth is a short ride from here. This small town lies tucked in the northern lee of the Black Mountains. It's clustered around a small square dominated by the memorial town clock. One of the early leaders of Methodism hailed from here and made a substantial impact on the eighteenth century religious revival. Howel Harris also founded a community in the nearby village of Trefeca. The town's name literally means 'end of the hills' and the Black Mountains are very much in evidence here. The fast flowing Ennig tumbles down a series of waterfalls through Pwll y Wrach nature reserve just above the town.

From Talgarth the road follows the lower reaches of the Llynfi, meandering between hedges, with the lower slopes of the mountains rising up to the south. The route rejoins the main road just before the village of Three Cocks. At **Glasbury** the Llynfi joins the Wye and a bridge leads across the river just below the confluence. The Wye here is the boundary between the counties of Brecon and Radnor and some buses now follow the north bank of the river and on to **Clyro**, renowned as the parish of Francis Kilvert. Kilvert was curate at Clyro between 1867 and 1872. From 1870 he wrote a diary about the life and people of the area, giving a fascinating picture of contemporary life and society. He mixed with all classes of people, including the gentry and the poor and his diary is still popular today. He also described the local landscape in detail and loved to walk across the hills of the area.

Hay is best known today for its panoply of second hand bookshops. In 1961 Richard Booth started trading books in Hay. Within a couple of decades he had not only built up his own business but had also nurtured the novel concept of a 'booktown', isolated from the great urban centres, but attracting a self-sustaining niche trade. Other towns have since followed this path, but nowhere perhaps as successfully as Hay. Booth's energy and flamboyance drove the unique form of rural regeneration forward with stunts such as declaring Hay independent and himself King on 1st April 1977. Today, Hay is home to an enormous variety of bookshops and to the Guardian Hay Festival of Literature, which takes place around the spring bank holiday each year.

From Hay the bus soon enters Herefordshire and England and travels into the **Golden Valley**, named after the river Dore, which sounds like d'or (golden) in French. You pass through the picturesque villages of Dorstone and Peterchurch. At Vowchurch, you leave the Golden Valley to head for Hereford by way of Kingstone. As you join the main road from Wales, the modern supermarket complex contrasts with the historic city just below you.

Hereford to Abergavenny

Hereford's Welsh name, Henffordd, means 'old road'. It is indeed situated at an ancient crossing of the Wye. The city is an old Saxon settlement and there has been a place of worship on the site of the cathedral for centuries. The tower is still the focus of the city's skyline. The building dates from Norman times but contains many other noteworthy features. The famous medieval map, the Mappa Mundi can be viewed here, as well as the unique chained library. The city is an important agricultural centre for the rich red soil of the county. The area produces beef from the famous Hereford cattle. It also grows hops and distinctive oast houses are used to dry these. This is also the heart of a fruit growing area and apples are used to produce cider. The Cider Museum and King Offa distillery explore the story of cider making in the area.

The road back into Wales climbs out of the city through the suburban area of Newton, retracing your route of entry. Instead of turning off towards the Golden Valley, the bus sticks to the main road, heading directly for Abergavenny. The country south-west of Hereford was for centuries a disputed area. Local place names are evidence of a distinctly Welsh lilt. The district was known in English as Archenfield and in Welsh as Ergyng depending on your preference. The Domesday Book refers to the disputed nature of the border marches. 'In **Archenfield** the king has three churches. The priests of these churches undertake the king's embassies into Wales, and each of them sings for the king two masses every week. When any one of them dies, the king customarily has 20 shillings from him. If any Welshman steals a man or a woman, a horse, an ox, or a cow, on being convicted, he first returns what has been stolen and [then] pays 20 shillings as a fine. If he kills any thegn's man, he gives 10 shillings to the lord of the slain man. But if a Welshman kills a Welshman, the relatives of the slain man come together and plunder the slayer and his kin and burn their houses until, toward noon on the following day, the body of the slain man is buried.' The phone box at Llanveynoe, a few miles west of the road but still in England, carries the title 'Teleffôn', showing that even BT is confused.

You enter Wales officially at **Pontrilas** and the border follows the river Monnow for the next few miles. This is a picturesque route through distinctive border country. Rivers meandering through fertile red soil, backed by wooded hills, adorned by fruit trees and colonised by timbered farmhouses. The profile of the **Skirrid**, or more properly Ysgyryd Fawr, lies ahead. It is one of the three peaks dominating the approaches to Abergavenny, the other two being the Blorenge and the Sugar Loaf. Steep rocky cliffs buttress the summit and a strange looking landslip lies to the west of the summit. There are many legends about the landslip and the Skirrid's strange shape. The best known story alleges that the mountain was rent in two at the time of Christ's crucifixion. The Skirrid is also known locally as St Michael's Mount and as the Holy Mountain. Farmers were known to collect soil from its slopes to cure ailing cattle. In fact, the landslip occurred at the time of the last ice age. The bus turns off the fast main road to serve the community of Maerdy as it approaches the market town of Abergavenny *(for more details see Journey T).*

Abergavenny to Brecon

The road from Abergavenny heads west up the Usk valley towards the heartland of Wales and as soon as you leave the town you enter the Brecon Beacons National Park. To the south, across the Usk, rises the Blorenge and beyond lie the iron and coalfields of the valleys. North of the road, the wooded slopes of the Sugar Loaf sweep up to its graceful conical summit. Such is the temperate climate of these southern facing hillsides that a commercial vineyard produces wine here. The Usk meanders through fertile meadows on its way from the heights of the mountains to its meeting with the salt waters of the Bristol Channel at Newport. Soon you enter the vast county of Powys and at Glangrwyney you cross the Grwyne, draining the heart of the Black Mountains. On the north side of the road are the extensive grounds of military training camp.

Crickhowell is an attractive town, marinated in history. A Norman castle, a fine bridge across the Usk and the fourteenth century parish church are just some of the features that give the town an air of permanence. Its name derives from the iron-age fort, situated just above the town to the north on a plateau known as Table Mountain. The location became known as Crug Hywel, the fort of Hywel, after Hywel Dda, Hywel the Good. A famous Welsh tenth century leader, grandson of Rhodri Mawr, Hywel is chiefly remembered for instituting a code of law which did much to unify the country.

At Nantyffin, an old AA box marks the parting of the ways. The road to Builth Wells and Mid Wales branches right up the Rhiangoll Valley. Our route stays on the A40. On the left a grey stone bridge carries a private road into Glanusk Park. A little further on you can glimpse the round tower of Tretower Castle through the trees across the fields. **Tretower** has always been at an important crossroads close to the confluence of the Usk and Rhiangoll. So perhaps it is unsurprising that there are two historic buildings on the same site. The thirteenth century stone keep superseded an early Norman castle. Next to it is a rare example of a late medieval manor house, its present form dating from the fifteenth century. Both are in the care of Cadw and are open to the public. The road now abandons the Usk valley, at least for a short while. The bus aims for the houses of Bwlch, straddling the narrow ridge ahead. It twists through the village passing over the saddle to descend back to the Usk. At Llansantffraed church, it turns south to **Talybont-on-Usk**, guarding the entrance to the Caer Fanell Valley. This carried the railway across the mountains to Merthyr and Cardiff. Nowadays the track is a cycle route, the Taff Trail. From Talybont, you follow the Monmouthshire and Brecon canal. A roundabout marks the beginning of the Brecon bypass, but our route takes us into the town passing a military training centre. The upper reaches of the canal accompany the road on the left, while on the opposite side the grey stone walls of the army barracks also house the South Wales Borderers Museum. You have completed an eighty mile round trip around the borderland mountains.

Route Information
!! Warning
The X43 is an amalgam of various transport needs, partly connected to the Brecon Beacons National Park. It is likely to face further change, or to be split into separate sections. There has been talk of a new direct service from Brecon to Newport via Abergavenny, and such a service existed

until a few years ago. Despite the detailed uncertainties, it is likely that there will be some kind of bus service between the points in this journey. Just watch out for changes of timetable, service number or operator.

Section	Bus No.	Operator	Weekday frequency	Sunday frequency	Jny Time	Rover tickets
Brecon - Hay - Hereford	39	Stagecoach in S Wales	7 journeys	2 journeys	1 hour 45 min	FPS NR
Hereford - Abergavenny*	X3 X4	Stagecoach in S Wales	Aprox hourly	No service	55 min	FPS NR
Abergavenny - Brecon**	X43	Sixty Sixty	Every 2 hours	No service	50 min	FPS

NOTES
* Service operates to/from Cardiff (See Journey T)
** Service operates to/from Merthyr and Cardiff (See Journey V)

Places to Visit

Brecon Cathedral   01874-623857

South Wales Borderers and Mon. Regt. Museum
                                          01874-613310
                                          www.rrw.org.uk

Hereford Cathedral   01432-374202
                                  www.herefordcathedral.org

Cider Museum and Offa Distillery, Hereford
                                          01432-354207
                                   www.cidermuseum.co.uk

Waterworks Museum, Hereford   01432-361147

Hereford Museum and Art Gallery   01432-260692
                                   www.herefordshire.gov.uk

Abergavenny Museum   01873-854282
                              www.monmouthshire.gov

Tretower Castle and Court   01874-730279
                              www.cadw.wales.gov.uk

Ideas for Walking

The Black Mountains offer many opportunities for walks of all kinds. It is possible to climb the Sugar Loaf from Abergavenny. Details of routes can be obtained from the National Park Information Centre next to the bus station. Offa's Dyke long distance path crosses the Black Mountains by traversing its most easterly ridge. The 17-mile route runs from Pandy, north of Abergavenny to Hay. With careful planning the bus routes on this journey can be used to return. (It's always easier to use the bus on the outward trip on linear walks, and then walk back to your starting point. It leaves less to chance.)

Refreshments

Hereford, Hay, Brecon, Abergavenny, Crickhowell and Talgarth all provide refreshments shops and other facilities. A browse among Hay's second-hand bookshops will be rounded off well with lunch or tea in one of the many restaurants or cafés in this small border town.

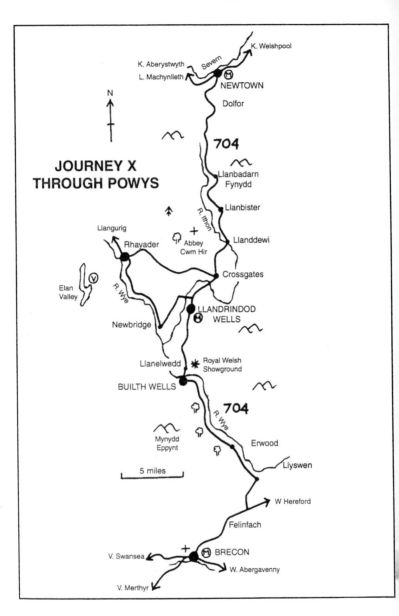

JOURNEY X
THROUGH POWYS

N

K. Welshpool
K. Aberystwyth
L. Machynlleth
Severn
NEWTOWN

Dolfor

704

Llangurig
Llanbadarn Fynydd

Rhayader
Llanbister

Abbey Cwm Hir
R. Ithon
Llanddewi

Elan Valley
Crossgates

LLANDRINDOD WELLS

Newbridge

R. Wye

Llanelwedd
Royal Welsh Showground

BUILTH WELLS

704
R. Wye

Mynydd Eppynt
Erwood

5 miles
Llyswen

W Hereford

Felinfach
BRECON

V. Swansea
W. Abergavenny
V. Merthyr

Journey X: Through Powys

Newtown – Llandrindod – Builth Wells – Brecon

This is the missing link. For many years it was difficult to find a coherent north-south bus service through Powys. Buses ran between Llandrindod to Brecon, and there was an irregular service covering various permutations between Newtown and Llandrindod. In early 2006, a new service was inaugurated under the TrawsCambria logo. This now provides a regular bus between Newtown and Brecon. Good links at either end of the route mean that travel down the eastern side of Wales is now a realistic possibility.

From Newtown the route climbs through attractive, hilly country. Dropping to Llanbadarn Fynydd, it follows the river Ithon to Llandrindod Wells, the county town of Powys and mid-point on the Heart of Wales railway line. Undulating pastoral country leads to Builth Wells, on the banks of the Wye and home to the Royal Welsh Showground. South of Builth, a pleasant road accompanies the twists of the Wye with the Black Mountains soon looming ahead. When the river turns northwest, our route goes in the opposite direction, crossing the watershed to reach the Usk valley at Brecon.

Newtown to Llandrindod Wells

Newtown is one of mid Wales' largest communities and stands astride the Severn and at the western terminus of the old Montgomery Canal. *(For details about Newtown see Journey L.)* From the town, the main road heads south and almost immediately begins to climb up out of the Severn valley. It's a gentle, but sinuous, ascent for several miles wandering between hedgerows and with views across the hills. In the hamlet of Dolfor a side road leads towards

Kerry Hill. Just along this road is the start of the ancient Kerry Ridgeway, an old drovers' route that ran east into England, never dipping below 1,000 feet. Its origins are lost in antiquity but it certainly predates the iron-age remains that have been built across it. It was last used for droving about 150 years ago. Walking south on Offa's Dyke you get your last view of the Berwyn range and your first of the Black Mountains as you cross the Ridgeway. Somehow between Newtown and Llandrindod, you similarly tilt from northern Wales into southern.

Past Dolfor the road sweeps to the right and becomes more level for a while. But it soon climbs again, this time up to the summit of the road and the watershed between Severn and Wye catchments. Although much of the country is enclosed, there's an atmosphere of wild isolation. It is not difficult to imagine the drovers herding sheep across the hills. You may catch a glimpse of the magnificent red kite, now a common presence in mid Wales. Buzzards, too, use the wilder uplands for hunting. Clumps of conifers are silhouetted against the horizon, while reedy patches mark the soggy marshes that gestate tiny streams which in turn feed the great rivers of Wales. Just across the old border from Montgomeryshire to Radnorshire, a myriad of such rivulets coalesce to form the infant Ithon, an important tributary of the Wye. The river soon carves a valley and the road faithfully follows each twist reaching the village of Llanbadarn Fynydd. The sides become steeper south of the village and trees cling to rocky crags. **Llanbister** gives its name to a station on the picturesque Heart of Wales railway line, though the station itself is a few miles east of the village. St Cynllo's church is built on a steep hillside, allowing a baptistry for full immersion to be built into the hillside, an unusual feature for an Anglican church. Although the church dates from the fourteenth century, its reredos, showing 'Christ in Majesty', is as recent as the 1950s.

The Ithon valley widens out south of Llanbister. Deep in a wooded valley a few miles west is **Abbey Cwm Hir**. This was the largest Cistercian abbey in Wales and only three English cathedrals, York, Durham and Winchester, beat the length of its nave. The abbey claims to be the burial place of last native Prince of Wales, Llywelyn ap Gruffudd. He was killed in an ambush a few miles away at Cilmeri in 1282. The monastery was dissolved in the sixteenth century, though only three monks remained at that time. The ruins of the abbey can still be explored.

At Crossgates, you cross the main A44 as it heads for the west coast at Aberystwyth. As you leave the village, the road passes beneath the Heart of Wales railway line and then leaves the company of the Ithon to head over undulating country into Llandrindod, spa town and administrative centre for the vast county of Powys.

Llandrindod Wells is an attractive and spacious spa town. The springs have been used for centuries; even the Romans seem to have known about them. It was in the eighteenth century that the spa developed with the discovery of sulphur and saline springs in 1732. A hotel opened a couple of decades later. Around 1830 Cook's Typography of Wales warned visitors that sulphurous water 'should on no account be taken in the afternoon.' But it was the arrival of the railway in 1865 that gave the impetus to Llandrindod's expansion and popularity. This lasted into the twentieth century until the spa was eventually closed in 1971. Since then it has reopened and is now a centre for complementary medicine. Today you can enjoy a pleasant walk in Rock Park, focused around its lake and its enigmatic 'beast' sculpture in the centre.

The remains of a medieval chapel, Capel Maelog, have been re-erected on the edge of the park. The National Cycling Exhibition is situated in a former garage and displays a variety of vintage and modern bicycles. The town is also the mid point on the Heart of Wales railway line and the Signal Box Museum offers an insight into life on the line. A Victorian festival is held annually in August.

Llandrindod to Brecon

Beyond Llandrindod a straighter road passes the village of Howey but it soon regains its curvaceous instinct as it undulates across the grain of the country. After a while it descends through woods to reach **Llanelwedd**, home of the Royal Welsh Showground. The ground hosts the Royal Welsh Show at the end of July and a number of other events during the year. Beyond Llanelwedd a bridge crosses the Wye into **Builth**. This is also the old county boundary between Radnorshire and Breconshire. The Normans built their first castle here in 1098 but Edward I later rebuilt it as a stone fortress at the end of the thirteenth century. Only a few earthworks remain today. Today Builth is a thriving market town and you can enjoy a pleasant stroll along the banks of the Wye.

From Builth, the A483 road turns west towards Llanwrtyd, Llandovery and Swansea. At **Cilmeri**, a few miles along the road, a memorial commemorates the death of Llywelyn, the last native-born Prince of Wales, in 1282. But our route leaves this road at Builth, instead turning east to take the trunk road towards Brecon and Cardiff. Soon the bulk of Aberedw Hill forces the river and road on to a southerly course. The road never strays far from the Wye as it descends, sometimes tumbling down rapids, sometimes flowing more sedately, like an uncertain adolescent. The road weaves gently along the floor of the valley between the Radnorshire Hills and Mynydd Epynt. The lower slopes are rich in trees and hedgerows, while higher up bracken hints at wilder high ground. Across the river, Aberedw is the site of an ancient motte castle, and today the focus for walks alongside the Wye or up into the extensive open common of Aberedw Hill. There's a craft centre just across the bridge at Erwood. A little way further on the valley broadens and here is the first clear view of the dramatic northern escarpment of the Black Mountains. This high ground forces the Wye northeast towards Hay and Hereford *(see Journey W)*. But our route turns west at Llyswen. The road now lies through undulating country past the village of Felinfach to cross the Wye-Usk watershed. It's not long before you drop down into the town of Brecon, built at the junction of the Usk and Honddu rivers. The Brecon Beacons now lie ahead, and beyond them the populous valleys of the south and the road to the capital. *(For more about Brecon see Journey V.)*

Links from Rhayader

Rhayader claims to be the oldest town in mid Wales, dating back 1500 years. It's the first town on the river Wye, set among magnificent mountains. The town is also gateway to the Elan Valley and the complex of reservoirs built to serve the West Midlands. This is wild life country. The Red Kite Centre lies at Gigrin Farm on the edge of the town and 150 kites are fed here daily. The Gilfach Nature Reserve lies a few miles to the north, just off the road to Llangurig. A reasonable bus service links Rhayader and Llandrindod via Newbridge on Wye or Crossgates. It is also possible to travel to Llangurig or Llanidloes (and therefore on to Aberystwyth) but services are patchy and eccentric so check first.

Route Information

Section	Bus No.	Operator	Weekday frequency	Sunday frequency	Jny Time	Rover tickets
Newtown - Brecon	704	Stagecoach in S Wales	Every 2 hours	No service	1 hour 55 min	FPS
Llandrindod-Rhayader	19	Various	6 journeys	No service	30 min	FPS

NOTE
Service 704 was introduced in 2006. It may be extended to Merthyr and Cardiff eventually.

Places to Visit

Robert Owen Memorial Museum, Newtown
01686-626345
www.robert-owen.midwales.com

WH Smith Museum, Newtown   01686-626280

Newtown Textile Museum   01686-622024

National Cycling Exhibition, Llandrindod 01597-825531

Radnorshire Museum, Llandrindod   01597-824513

Red Kite Feeding Station, Rhayader   www.gigrin.co.uk

Gilfach Nature Reserve   01597-870301
www.westwales.co.uk/gilfach.htm

Erwood Station Craft Centre   01982-553307
www.erwood-station.co.uk

Brecon Cathedral   01874-623857

South Wales Borderers and Mon. Regt. Museum
                                                  01874-613310

Ideas for Walking
The Wye Valley Walk follows the route from Builth to
Llyswen, a distance of about 12 miles. It offers a more
intimate acquaintance with the river, perhaps with a stop
at the Erwood Station Craft Centre.

Refreshments
Both Llandrindod and Builth offer convenient stopovers.
Builth is particularly attractive and its narrow main street
provides a number of venues for lunch or an evening
meal.